trotman

GETTING INTO THE UK'S BEST UNIVERSITIES AND COURSES

BERYL DIXON

The Daily Telegraph

Getting into the UK's Best Universities & Courses

This first edition published in 2008 by Trotman Publishing, a division of Crimson Publishing Ltd., Westminster House, Kew Road, Richmond, Surrey TW9 2ND

© Trotman Publishing 2008

Author: Beryl Dixon

Designed by Andy Prior

British Library Cataloguing in Publication Data
A catalogue record for this book is available from the British Library

ISBN 978-1-84455-179-8

Typeset by Newgen Imaging Systems Pvt Ltd.
Printed and bound in Great Britain by MPG Books Ltd, Bodmin

GETTING INTO THE UK'S BEST UNIVERSITIES AND COURSES

Contents

ACKNOWLEDGEMENT	VII
INTRODUCTION	1
CHAPTER ONE – Why choose a high-ranking university or course?	9
CHAPTER TWO – Planning your application	17
CHAPTER THREE – Choosing your course and institution	33
CHAPTER FOUR – Maximising your chances	57
CHAPTER FIVE – What are they looking for?	71
CHAPTER SIX – Admissions tests	91
CHAPTER SEVEN – Interviews and auditions	105
CHAPTER EIGHT – Offers and rejections	127
CHAPTER NINE – Results day	133
CHAPTER TEN – Postscript	141

ACKNOWLEDGEMENTS

I would like to thank all the people who agreed to be featured in this book and to say an especial Thank You to Stella Barnes of Queen Elizabeth Sixth Form College, Darlington and Anne Lispscombe of Slough Grammar School, both hardworking careers advisers who know all that there is to know about applying to higher education and who helped me to identify some of the students who appear as case studies in the book.

INTRODUCTION

This book is written for students in Years 12 and 13 (or lower and upper sixth according to the definitions used in your school or college) who are starting to think about higher education. Students in earlier years may also find it relevant if they are starting to think about higher education.

It is not a magic guide to getting into Oxford, Cambridge or any other high status university. There are no special tricks, as you will realise every time the press comes up with another story regarding a star student who has been denied a place at an excellent university. Is it prejudice against private schools? Against grammar schools? Rejection by left wing academics etc. Or is it simply bad luck? Well, logic tells us that if high numbers of applicants are going to choose the same universities or courses, more of them have to be unsuccessful, however careful the selection process.

So that is about what the book is not. What are its aims then?

Quite simply to help you as far as possible to find a place on a good course. You will notice that I say 'course'. That is because even a 'good' university can have one or two weak courses. And not all good courses are in universities. Some are in colleges. You wouldn't necessarily go to a university offering an academic course in drama if you wanted to be a performer for instance – although some people do and come up through the route of student drama societies. Similarly, most well known artists – unless completely self-taught – have attended an art school. Few of these are now freestanding but have been absorbed into nearby universities. The point is though that these universities are not always the ones considered to be in the A list. Vocational courses – that is those leading to a career or career area, including some in popular subject areas like automobile design, fashion, marketing – are in B list establishments. The same applies to some of the degree courses that train students in the health care professions.

You can't do journalism at Bristol, physiotherapy at Cambridge, accountancy at Oxford or pharmacy at Sheffield – but these are all highly-rated universities where you can apply to do lots of other courses.

What's all this about A list and B list places? You can't have failed to notice that some universities have higher status than others and that some are regarded as second class. How do you attempt to rate them? There are all kinds of ways, some of them very unscientific – and do you know the phrase 'Lies, damned lies and statistics? I'm not saying that statistics are not valid but before you start to look at them you have to know what *you* are looking for and what *they* are measuring.

You could assume for instance that the best universities are the ones that attract the most applicants. I did a very unscientific survey, using figures from UCAS, the organisation that handles applications to UK higher education courses, which show the numbers of applications received by every university and college by the advisory closing date of 15th January 2008. This refers to applications for courses beginning in autumn 2008 and it means applications not applicants (each applicant can make up to five applications). I chose an arbitrary figure of 25,000+ applications and came up with the following list of universities:

- Birmingham
- Bristol
- Cardiff
- Edinburgh
- King's College, London
- Kingston
- Leeds
- Leeds Metropolitan
- Manchester
- Manchester Metropolitan
- Nottingham
- Sheffield
- Sheffield Hallam
- Southampton
- Ulster
- University College, London (UCL)
- Warwick.

When I dropped to 20,000 applications the following were added:

- Brighton
- Durham
- Exeter
- Glasgow
- Liverpool
- Liverpool John Moore's
- Newcastle
- Nottingham Trent
- West of England (in Bristol).

So does that give us the top 26 universities? There are one or two important ones missing are there not? What about Oxford with only 14,092 applications and Cambridge with 14,494? Have they declined in popularity? There are one or two other Russell Group (see page 4 for a definition) universities are missing too. Where are Imperial College, London, the London School of Economics and Queen's University, Belfast? Do students prefer to live in large cities? What is wrong with the North East or the far South West of England?

No – the above is not a complete list of 'good' universities and there are some simple reasons why not. I didn't look at size of institution or at how many and which courses they offer. It stands to reason that a specialist drama school is going to draw applicants from a very small pool – and you can bet your life that most of them will be talented, thus increasing the competition for places – compared to a large university offering almost every course possible. I didn't count how many applications in total were made to universities and colleges which are not in large cities. (There are 314 universities and colleges in the UCAS scheme and many are in small towns or in rural locations.) I didn't take into account the fact that London may be popular with international students, as may be other cities they have heard of. I didn't consider the fact that some universities attract a lot of local applicants who prefer not to leave their home areas. All these factors influence choice. And I didn't allow for the fact that the numbers applying to Oxford and Cambridge are self-selecting – or selected. Schools and colleges normally only recommend students to apply to these two universities if they have a strong chance of getting in.

I could have found a different list if I had checked on entry grades required (making the assumption that if these are high the status of the university must also be so), employment rates of graduates, number of first class honours degrees awarded, percentage of students who can be accommodated in halls of residence or numbers of books in the library.

I have mentioned the Russell Group. What is this? It's an exclusive club of 20 universities that gets its name from the London hotel where representatives of these universities first met to set up the group. They are 'research-led' universities which means that their staff produce research which is highly rated in research assessment exercises and that they teach postgraduates as well as undergraduates. They sometimes speak as a group on matters such as entry requirements, entry standards and so on, as you will see when you get to Chapter 4. The members are:

- Birmingham
- Bristol
- Cambridge
- Cardiff
- Edinburgh
- Glasgow
- Imperial College, London
- King's College, London
- Leeds
- Liverpool
- London School of Economics and Political Science (LSE)
- Manchester
- Newcastle
- Nottingham
- Queen's University Belfast
- Oxford
- Sheffield
- Southampton
- UCL
- Warwick.

For many people this is the A list. They are often referred to in the media as the 'group of leading universities' and because of this they can ask for high entry grades and attract some very well-qualified applicants. But even some of the most demanding universities have lower requirements for some of their courses. It all depends on how many applications they receive. I have worked on far more A level results days than I care to remember, trying to come up with alternatives for students who had not achieved the grades they had been asked to get. Time and time again one department in a university would refuse to budge from AAB while another in the same university would happily drop two grades in order to fill the course.

However, you do not need to go to a highly rated university to receive a good education and to get a good job. There some employers who prefer to recruit students from prestigious establishments but there also those who prefer to recruit from universities whose courses they know and where they may have links with students through work experience or sponsorship. And – you might be relieved to know   there are others who do not worry too much about where students went as much as what they learned there and what skills they have.

How do we define 'best course'? There is no such thing really. Let's say 'popular' instead. If a course appeals to you the chances are that it attracts numbers of other students too. There is more competition for places on some courses than on others. If a course attracts a lot of applicants it will be more difficult to get on to. Selectors have to cut down the numbers somehow. Grades required will be high. High academic references will be expected. Certain A level/Diploma/Higher subjects may be required. (The Russell Group has recently made a statement regarding subjects some of its members do not like. You can see this in Chapter 4.)

In fact this book should really be called *Getting into the UK's Most Popular Courses.*

What it boils down to is that choosing a university or college is a very personal choice. Different people are happy or unhappy at different places. You need to go to the one that offers the best course for your requirements, your personality and your future success. This may sound like a cop out if you were expecting to be told which places really are the best but it's true.

There are numerous annual league tables that try to tell you which universities and subjects are the best ones. As with statistics you need to know what you are looking for. If they don't use your own criteria they are no good to you. They do use different factors to produce their ratings. A few years ago UCAS produced a book *How to Read League Tables*. In it the author pointed out that league tables produced by four different newspapers ranked the same university in 56th, 61st, 103rd and 163rd place! Nevertheless, most of you will probably want to look at them, so we'll do that in Chapter 3.

This book then is really about maximising your chances of getting in to the place you want to go to do the subject that you really want to do. There is nothing particularly unusual about the advice given but I have tried to draw together some tried and tested tips together with up-to-date advice from some admissions tutors – the people who select students for courses. Also included throughout the book are experiences of students who have gone through the process very recently. Some of them have made their applications this year and when this book was being researched did not yet know whether they would achieve the right exam results to take up their places. Others are now at university or college but can remember very well what they had to do to get there.

Chapter 1 – Why choose a high-ranking university or course?

This chapter covers the benefits of going to one of the top universities and/or courses in terms of future employment prospects. How can you find out which courses are most respected within an industry you may know that you want to work in?

Chapter 2 – Planning your application

This chapter gives an overview of the timescale for higher education applications and the various application methods for different courses. Deadlines may be earlier than you think. The different ways of applying for art and design courses are covered as are the procedures for music and drama courses.

Chapter 3 – Choosing your course and institution

This chapter outlines the key considerations when making your university and course choice. It also includes information on league tables and recommends all the sources of information that you will need. How do you find out this information? How reliable is the information?

Chapter 4 – Maximising your chances

This chapter, gives some suggestions on strategies you could adopt in the year before you apply (or even earlier) that could give your application an edge.

Chapter 5 – What are they looking for?

The top courses will be looking for specific qualities in their applicants. What are these? Will admissions tutors want to see evidence of work experience in applicants to specific courses? How can you go about getting this? This chapter tries to provide some of the answers.

Chapter 6 – Admissions tests

Selection for some top courses is no longer done on the basis of exam results alone. This chapter covers the additional exams or essays that may be required as well as the aptitude tests that are now almost obligatory for law and medicine.

Chapter 7 – Interviews and auditions

Many admissions tutors no longer have the time to interview. Others, particularly if their course leads to a professional qualification, see the interview or audition part of selection as very important. This chapter discusses the types of interview and interview questions you might expect, with some tips on preparing for them.

Chapter 8 – Offers and rejections

There is information here on how offers of places or (unfortunately) rejections can be made and what to do if this happens.

Chapter 9 – Results day

An overview of what should happen on results day. This covers the procedures if you get your grades and what to do if you miss your grades. **Clearing** is explained here.

Chapter 10 – Postscript

One last point. It's going to be quite tedious if I keep saying 'university, college or school'. 'Institution' sounds like a prison. So from now on I am going to adopt the term used by some other guides to higher education application – higher education institution, HEI for short.

CHAPTER ONE
WHY CHOOSE A HIGH-RANKING UNIVERSITY OR COURSE?

Does an HEI's status matter to you? If it does, you will probably want to look at the information in Chapter 3 which looks at the different ways in which universities and colleges are rated. The problem is though that different league tables use different criteria when comparing them, as you will have read in the Introduction. But if you are interested in HEIs' general overall reputation you will find that the same eight or ten names crop up in all the tables, whatever their methods of compilation.

However, when it comes to comparing HEIs for different subjects a different picture can emerge. In an article in *The Education Guardian* on 1st May 2008 some interesting points were made regarding the position of some new universities in *The Guardian's* league tables, namely:

- The University of Bedfordshire (formerly Luton) was in third place for media and communication studies.
- Bath and Loughborough were first and second in sports science.
- Bournemouth and Brighton Universities were rated first and second in tourism.
- Oxford Brookes was in first place for social work
- Sussex was first for chemistry.

None of these is a Russell Group university.

If you are going to put your efforts into finding out about well-respected HEIs and/ or courses, you need to ask yourself first – what do you mean by a high-ranking HEI? Is it one at which you will receive good teaching? (See Chapter 3 again.) Or do you mean one which should help you to get a good job? I suspect the latter. And it is very likely that this is the criterion that is most important to parents.

Does it really matter whether or not you graduate from an A list university? Yes, if you want to work for a top law firm, blue chip company or financial institution like an investment bank or major insurance company. Some employers recruit only from their own list of preferred universities. If therefore you find a course that you like at a high status university, go for it. However, you must bear in mind that the more popular places are able to demand higher entry grades. Indeed many do so not because their course is more difficult than others but as one way of cutting out some of their applicants.

SOME EMPLOYERS

If you know at this stage what your career is to be and you also know of some employers you would like to work for, you can go directly to their websites, search under 'Graduate Recruitment' or 'Careers' and see whether they have any preferences. For example if you visit the Rolls-Royce website you will find that representatives from the company attend careers fairs or give presentations at the following universities:

- Aston
- Bath
- Birmingham
- Bristol
- Cambridge
- Cardiff
- Durham
- Imperial
- LSE
- Loughborough
- Manchester
- Nottingham
- Oxford
- Sheffield
- Southampton
- Strathclyde
- Warwick.

This does *not* mean that students from other HEIs are not accepted. But it does suggest that Rolls-Royce has found suitable applicants in the past from the ones listed and is keen to maintain contact.

If you look on www.wikijob.co.uk you will find certain universities suggested as being the best for people who hope to enter investment banking. Twenty are listed but the advice is that the majority of successful applicants come one of those in the top seven, which are:

1.	Cambridge
2.	Imperial
3.	King's College, London
4.	LSE
5.	Oxford
6.	UCL
7.	TWarwick

The LSE is held to be particularly beneficial 'as it provides numerous networking opportunities from young investment banker alumni. LSE also has an investment society and a business society. In both cases, students receive regular talks directly from investment banks about careers, opportunities and applying.'

This is the sort of information you can find for yourself by using websites such as job-related ones like wikijob or from companies' and organisations' own sites.

You can also get, or ask for, information regarding employment from HEIs themselves. Many include it on their websites or in their prospectuses. If it is not there, you may email or write to ask for the information. Recent destination lists are what you want. George Peck, who is a drama school principal, suggests looking at how many students from the last two years are in work and what they are doing.

The Careers Services in all HEIs are required to contact students six months after they leave and ask what they are doing. There are two problems here however. Response rates are not always good. Students tend to bin question-naires from former HEIs or forget about them. And – six months is far too early. Many students are still in temporary jobs at that point – or are travelling. Even so, many Careers Services do manage to gather very useful information.

A second source is the department where students studied. Many of them manage to find out where their past students are and they publish this information (especially if it is good and they can include some impressive destinations).

You might be able to find career information on HEIs **Entry Profiles** on the UCAS website. One standard heading is 'What can this course offer me?', under this there is often a subheading 'Careers Information'.

Here are some sample entries.

A: Careers followed by graduates with Mathematics degrees

The university's Careers Service contacts maths graduates six months after they get their degrees. By then, over 90% of those seeking work have found it, the majority in well-paid professions with starting salaries up to £30,000, and occasionally even higher in demanding areas of banking. The detailed records kept by the Careers Service show two clear things about our mathematicians:

- the sheer variety of professions open to them
- their penetration in certain key areas of the economy like finance and IT.

First destinations

Statistics gathered by the Careers Service on the first employment taken by our mathematics graduates can be found on their Web pages. Follow the link under 'This year's data' and click on 'Mathematics' to download a three-page summary as a Word document.

B: What are the career opportunities?

Graduates from the School of Mathematics are much in demand for a wide variety of jobs and are less likely to be unemployed than the graduate population as a whole, with most finding permanent employment in due course. Here is a brief summary of the first destinations of our mathematics students six months after they graduated:

- Permanent Employment 64
- Further Study/Training 38
- Still Seeking Employment/Studying/Training 17
- Not available for Employment/Studying/Training 5.

These figures are from the 124 graduates (out of 161 contacted) who responded to a request for information.

As you can see, over 85% of all the graduates who returned information are either employed, undertaking further study, or are not available for work (which usually means they are spending the year after graduation travelling or doing voluntary work overseas). The most popular areas of employment are actuarial/accountancy/banking (20 responses), other financial and admin/management work (18) or computer related activity (3); but the above figures show that postgraduate study and teacher training are also very popular career choices.

C: Career opportunities

The programme aims to equip you personally and educationally for a variety of careers and activities by developing both critical faculties and transferable skills. Recent English graduates have been successful in obtaining employment in the media, journalism, publishing, the theatre, arts administration, teaching, industry, commerce, law, computing, accountancy, personnel and social work. Many graduates go on to postgraduate study.

As one of a select list of schools offering IEE-accredited MEng programmes, our degrees fulfil the educational requirements for Chartered Engineer (CEng) status. This is the standard qualification required for many research engineering posts, and carries international recognition with other national institutes.

As a long-established research-led university, we carry a high level of recognition in the UK and abroad. Because of the school's close links with industry, our degrees are directly relevant to employment needs. Recent graduates have been employed by companies such as Sharp, British Aerospace, Pace, Fitronic, BNFL, AEAT Rail, Rover and the BBC. Opportunities exist both in large multi-national corporations as well as small start-up companies working on the next generations technologies.

As you will see the **Entry Profile** details vary in quantity and quality. These four entries are from HEIs that provide them. Unfortunately, not all HEIs do so – and when they do, they do not all use the same headings.

What else should you know?

PROFESSIONAL RECOGNITION

Some professions have entry requirements that may influence your choice of HEI.

Some examples:

- If you wish to enter the legal profession and become a barrister (advocate in Scotland) or solicitor you will need to undertake further professional training. This will be shorter if your degree is what is known as a *qualifying law degree*. You can check this with HEIs. The Law Society (for England and Wales) also has a list of qualifying degrees on its website. This allows you to check whether certain two-subject degrees, such as Law with Chemistry or Law and English are recognised.
- It is necessary to take further training in order to achieve chartered engineer status. This is referred to in **Entry Profile** entry D where the HEI states that its degree is recognised by the professional body concerned (in this case the Institution of Electrical Engineers).
- Should you wish to become a chartered psychologist you should take a degree that includes a number of compulsory modules recognised by the British Psychological Society.
- There are some Journalism and Media degrees that are approved by the National Council for the Training of Journalists or the Periodicals Training Council. It is not essential to have one of these but if you want to consider the possibility of cutting down further training time or of being exempted from certain professional exams, you could check these out now.

There are many more examples and it is wise to do some research.

I said in the Introduction that we should really be talking about *popular* rather than *best*. The Introduction contained a list of the HEIs that fit that category. What about courses?

According to figures released on 14th February 2008 by UCAS, the **top ten** most popular subjects were:

1.	Law
2.	Medicine
3.	Psychology
4.	English
5.	Management Studies
6.	Nursing
7.	Training Teachers
8.	Combinations with Business and Administrative Studies
9.	History
10.	Business Studies.

Three of those course titles are very similar (e.g. Management and Business) so here are the next two in the popularity stakes:

1.	Sports Science
2.	Economics.

After that come Drama, Social Work and Computer Science.

The complete **top 20** were:

1.	Law
2.	Medicine
3.	Psychology
4.	English
5.	Management Studies
6.	Nursing
7.	Training Teachers
8.	Combinations with Business and Administrative Studies
9.	History
10.	Business Studies

1	Sports science
2	Economics
3	Drama
4	Social Work
5	Computer Science
6	Design Studies
7.	Combinations of Social Studies/Business/Law with Arts/Humanities
8	Combinations of Languages with Arts/Humanities
9	Mathematics
0	Combinations of Science/Engineering with Arts/Humanities/Languages.

CHAPTER TWO

PLANNING YOUR APPLICATION

You will apply for almost all courses in higher education through one central organisation, the Universities' and Colleges' Application Service, known as UCAS (or sometimes written as Ucas in the press). UCAS handles applications to degree, Foundation degree and Higher Diploma courses including Nursing Diplomas. (If you hear anyone talking about NMAS they are out of date. NMAS, which used to manage applications for Diplomas in nursing, ceased to exist in October 2007.) If anyone mentions ADAR or the Art and Design Admissions Registry they are even more behind the times as ADAR has been dead for years. However, anyone who is not bang up-to-date – and this can include relatives and even people who have left university recently – may not have heard of CUKAS (The Conservatoires UK Admission Services). This organisation came into being to deal with applications to certain music courses for entry from 2006 onwards. Its service is described further on in this chapter.

There are other exceptions to the 'Everything through UCAS' rule. If you want to apply to any freestanding drama schools for instance – that is ones that are not attached to a university or other HEI – you will need to get their own application forms. The same applies to Art Foundation Courses or as they are officially known, Level 3 Diplomas in Foundation Studies (Art & Design). Here again you will need individual application forms.

UCAS
UCAS is based in Cheltenham and acts on behalf of all its member HEIs, which pay a fee for the services. Its staff act as agents. They do not make any decisions on your application. That role is for admissions staff in the HEIs. UCAS relays their decisions to you between your application and enrolment on a course and helps with any problem or questions you have – concerning the applications procedure only.

There are two kinds of UCAS application – Route A and Route B. As Route B is specifically for art and design applications it is covered in a separate section in this chapter.

You can apply for up to five courses simultaneously in any one 'applications cycle' and there is an application fee of £15 (or £5 if you apply for only one course). You may make only one application and any attempts to beat the system by applying twice will immediately be spotted by the UCAS computer.

Important exceptions

- You may apply to four courses only in any one of medicine, dentistry and veterinary medicine/veterinary science.
- You may apply to three courses only through Route B Art and Design (more on this route later).

Route A or standard applications – when are they made?

It's normal to make your UCAS application well before you want to start your course. The usual period for making applications is from 1st September to 15th January in the academic year before your course is due to start. So for courses beginning in autumn 2009 application must be made between 1st September 2008 and 15th January 2009. You really should try to get the application in by the 15th January deadline, although HEIs may consider your application after this date. (They are not obliged to do so however, and may have already offered what they consider to be the right number of places.) It is actually advisable to get the application in well before the January deadline if you can. Admissions tutors begin to read them as they arrive. They do not keep them all on hold until 15th January. As they read the first ones they can spend a bit more time on them and may be more willing to be slightly flexible over entry grade requirements for applicants they consider suitable. In the peak period just after Christmas when applications arrive in droves they will have less discretion to do this, having already offered many places.

There are some exceptions though. **Some courses have earlier deadlines.** If you want to apply to any course at Oxford or Cambridge or to courses in medicine, dentistry or veterinary medicine or veterinary science your deadline will be 15th October. The relevant medicine, dentistry and veterinary medicine/

science courses are those with course codes A100, A101, A103, A104, A105, A106 and A300 (Medicine); A200, A201, A202, A203, A204, A205, A206 and A400 (Dentistry); and D100 or D101 for veterinary medicine or veterinary science courses.

Oxford applications

If you want to include this university in your application you will also need to complete an additional application form at the same time as you do the main UCAS application. In the past all applicants to Cambridge also were asked to submit a Cambridge Application Form in addition to a UCAS application. However, it is planned that applicants from the UK and EU for 2009 entry (or deferred entry in 2010) will only need to submit a UCAS application in order to apply to Cambridge.

N.B. You may not apply to both Cambridge and Oxford in the same year.

Law, medicine and dentistry

Most universities ask you to take a special entrance test (at around the same time as you submit your UCAS application). You will need to make sure that you know if you have to take them. Some also ask applicants for veterinary science to take one of the medical aptitude tests.

Please see Chapter 6 for a description of these tests and important information on deadlines for taking them.

Some universities set their own tests in popular subjects like history or English. Again, you'll need to check whether and when you must do them.

How to apply

UCAS uses an online application system known as **Apply**. You can access **Apply** from any computer that has internet access – so you can do different bits of the application at different times. Your application is stored by UCAS and will appear each time you log on. You will be able to change any of the information that you have entered until you are satisfied with it and are ready to submit it. You may want to begin or do some of it at your school or college but you could equally well choose to do so at home or in a library or other online centre.

There are around 900 online centres in the UK where you can view the UCAS website and make your application. You will not be charged a fee by the centre. You can find your nearest centre by looking on the UCAS website where they are listed under the following regions:

- East of England
- East Midlands
- Greater London
- North East
- North West
- Northern Ireland
- Scotland
- South East
- South West
- Wales
- West Midlands
- Yorkshire and Humberside.

How do you log on? By using a 'buzzword' given to you by your school or college. (it is the same one for all applicants from that centre). If you are an independent candidate – i.e. not at a school or college you can get a buzzword from a careers or Connexions centre and use that organisation as your application centre. Alternatively you can obtain a buzzword direct from UCAS. The first time you enter your buzzword you will be asked to choose a unique username and password which you need to enter each time. You will also be asked four security questions.

N.B. There are some technical requirements that your computer must comply with:

- You must use Internet Explorer version 5 or higher OR Netscape Navigator 6 or higher.
- Your browser must have JavaScript enabled.
- It must also have 128-bit encryption enabled.
- Your monitor must be at least 15 inches in size.
- The display must be set to 256 colours minimum.
- The screen must be set to a resolution of 800x600 or above.

Schools, colleges and careers/Connexions centres should have suitable computers. If you are using your home one you might need to check the manual.

You can choose to do your application in either English or Welsh.

There are online instructions for each section and **Apply** also has Help sections on each page which should help you with any points you are unsure of. If you cannot find the answers there you can contact the UCAS Customer Service Unit on 0871 468 0468.

The application contains the following sections:

- Registration
- Personal Details
- Additional Information (UK applicants only)
- Choices
- Education
- Employment
- Personal Statement
- Reference
- Declaration
- Pay and Send.

Registration

In this first section you are asked to give your name, address and date of birth. The system then gives you your username and you choose your password. From now on whenever you log in you will have to give this.

Personal details

You will see some of these already completed – copied there from the registration section you have completed. Now is the time to check that they are correct. Here you are asked for additional information such as nationality and any disabilities you may have.

If you make a mistake here **Apply** will note this and ask you to correct it.

Additional information

This section is for UK applicants only and asks for more personal details like ethnic origin. Some people see this as irrelevant; others see it as sensitive, but this information will not affect your chances of getting a place in any way. It is intended to help UCAS and HEIs monitor equal opportunities.

Choices

This where you list the courses and HEIs of your choice. It does not matter which order you put them in as you cannot express a preference anyway. The system will put them into alphabetical order later. You do need though, to give the HEIs' names and institution codes and the course code. If you put the wrong code in any place **Apply** will again alert you. This is possible. Lots of applicants have been known to apply to the wrong HEI or to put say the code for engineering when they meant business studies. In this section you must also state whether you are applying for deferred entry (i.e. you are applying now but want to take a gap year).

Education

Here you give the schools or colleges you have attended and all the relevant qualifications you have achieved plus the ones you are taking.

Employment

In this section, you put the details of any jobs you have had. You can leave this section blank, but including them could be helpful (see TIPS).

Personal Statement

This statement tells your chosen HEIs why you are applying for the courses you have chosen and what makes you a good applicant. It is the only section of the application that wants something other than facts from you and it gives you the chance to sell yourself. It can be very important. See Chapter 5 for advice on how to complete this part of the application.

Reference

Your application must contain a reference from someone who is able to write about you and your suitability for the course. The usual people to ask are personal tutors, form teachers, heads of year or careers advisers. If you are at a school or college whoever is in charge of the UCAS applications will tell you who to ask. This section of the application will then be completed before it is sent. If you are not applying through a school or college you should first approach a potential referee, get their agreement to provide a reference and ask them to send it to you so that you can paste it in to this section.

Declaration
When you have filled in each section and marked it as complete you need to read the declaration and confirm that you agree to its terms.

Pay and Send
There are different ways of dealing with this section. Most applicants pay here online, using a credit or debit card. Some schools and colleges though, have an arrangement under which they make one payment to UCAS on behalf of all their applicants. They will tell you if this is the case.

That's it. The application now goes to UCAS for processing.

 TIPS

■ Be sure that you have read Chapter 3 before you begin.

■ Have all the information you will need – exam results, details of jobs and employers, dates of attendance at different schools if relevant, names of HEIs and course codes all ready and to hand before you start the first sections.

■ Do give details of any jobs you have had – even holiday or weekend ones. Admissions staff like to know about these. There is more information on this aspect in Chapters 4 and 5.

■ Print off hard copies at different stages of the application and check them. It's easier to read through and revise text on paper.

■ Don't use the 'save password' option. Yes, it would save you having to key your password in each time BUT anyone using the same computer would be able to access your application and change it!

■ Don't give your password details to anyone. Write them down and keep them in a safe place.

■ It is a good idea to name someone who can act on your behalf regarding your application in case you became ill or temporarily unable to respond to correspondence from UCAS during the application period. There is a space on the application for you to do so.

■ Print off and keep a paper copy of the application so that you can have it in front of you if you need to contact either UCAS or an HEI about any points.

After you apply

When UCAS receives your completed application their staff process it, send a copy to each of your chosen HEIs and send you a Welcome Letter and important information. This includes confirmation of the courses and HEIs you have applied to. If this is incorrect you should contact UCAS at once to correct it. You will also be given a Personal ID, application number and **Track** username and password (new ones to note and remember!). **Track** is an online tracking system that allows you to check the progress of your application and HEIs' decisions whenever you wish to do so. Some applicants did so several times each day last year! You are often asked for your application number if you ring UCAS or HEIs. Don't worry about forgetting it. You'll soon have it off by heart.

Route B applications (Art and Design)

The difference for Route B applications is that, rather than going to up to five HEIs at the same time your application is sent to each of your selected institutions sequentially. So in this route you have to list your courses in order of preference. Only if you are not accepted by your first choice does your application go to the next, and so on.

Applications for this route are accepted between 1st September and 24th March. The reason for the later closing date is that many applicants will be on Foundation Courses in Art and Design and they need time to decide on their specialisations and prepare their portfolios. UCAS advises that you should get the application in before the closing date and suggests that you do so by 7th March.

You may make only **three** choices – and you must put these in order of first, second and third choice.

UCAS sends your applications at certain dates. Your first choice HEI will decide whether to invite you for an interview and then whether to make you an offer. If you decide to accept the offer, UCAS automatically cancels your other choices. If you do not receive an offer or decide to decline it, your application is sent to your second choice, and if necessary, to your third.

Combining Routes A and B

You will have read earlier that you may makeup to five choices. So, although you may apply to three courses only through Route B, you may make up your total number of applications up to five by using two Route A courses.

However, you do not have to make three Route B applications. As long as you do not exceed five courses in total and three Route B ones as a maximum, your combination of courses could be any of:

- Three Route B plus up to two Route A
- Two Route B plus up to three Route A
- One Route B plus up to four Route A.

How do you do this?

If you decide to apply for a mixture of Route A and Route B courses, you can apply for Route A as normal before 15th January and add your Route B choices later. This must be done before the Route B deadline of 24th March. The UCAS application has a question that asks whether you will want to add Route B choices. If you answer 'Yes' you will be able to add them and give an interview preference through **Track**.

There is a comprehensive flow chart to help you understand this process in the Overview of Applications section of the UCAS website: www.ucas.com/students/startapplication/apply/applyoverview.

UCAS CALENDAR PLUS ACTION PLAN

These dates are from 2007/8 but do not usually vary from year to year.

DATE	EVENT
1st September	**UCAS forms accepted from now.** Apply as soon as you are ready. The earlier the better – admissions tutors start to make offers as they read application forms. They do **not** wait until the closing date. BUT don't hurry and cut corners. Take time to choose courses carefully and write a good personal statement.
15th October	**Closing date for applications for medicine, dentistry, veterinary medicine/science and for any course at Oxford or Cambridge (including the Ruskin School of Drawing and Fine Art – the Fine Art department of Oxford University).** Make sure the person who will be writing your reference knows that you need to meet this deadline and give your form to him or her in plenty of time. They will be under pressure at this time of year with numerous references to write.
1st January	**Art and Design Route B applications now accepted.** Don't forget – you may have only three choices (but are allowed to make two more through Route A).
15th January	**Closing Date for applications – including Art and Design Route A.** You may still apply, but your application will be regarded as 'Late' and universities and colleges will not be obliged to consider you. **However**, if you are applying from outside the EU you have until 30th June before you are classed as a late applicant – with the exception of the courses with the 15th October deadline. This one still applies.
26th February to 7th July	If you are not holding any offers you will have the opportunity to make an additional choice from places still available. This is done through the UCAS **Extra** service. Ask advice at school or college as to whether you should accept any offer received under this scheme or wait for main **Clearing**.

7th March	**Recommended deadline for Art and Design Route B applications.** You may still apply later – but places will be filling quickly. Is your portfolio ready? Expect to be invited to interviews soon.
24th March	Art and Design Route B applications received now will be considered late but will still be forwarded.
May	If you applied by the 15th January for the main UCAS scheme (including Art and Design Route A) you should receive final decisions from all the colleges and universities you applied to and must now reply. You may accept one offer as a **Firm Acceptance** and one as an **Insurance Acceptance**. Think carefully, then reply to UCAS. **N.B.** Some people may have had all five decisions before this date and will have replied already.
12th June	Route B applications received after this date will now have to wait until **Clearing**. Find out how **Clearing** works! See Chapter 9.
30th June	All other applications, including Art and Design Route A received after this date will go into **Clearing**. Find out about **Clearing**!
July	If you applied between 16th January and 30th June for the main UCAS scheme (including Art and Design Route A) you should have by now received final decisions.
7th July	Last date to use **Extra**.
Mid-August	**Clearing** begins.

ADDITIONAL INFORMATION FOR ROUTE B APPLICANTS

DATE	EVENT
12th February	UCAS starts to send early applications to first choice HEIs.
28th March	Second round applications are sent out from this date.

9th May	Last date for first choice to HEIs make their decisions.
23rd May	Third round applications are sent out from this date.
6th June	Last date for second choice to HEIs make their decisions.
7th July	Last date for third choice to HEIs make their decisions.
Mid-July	**Clearing** begins.

CUKAS

Conservatoires UK Admissions Service (CUKAS) is the admissions service
for places at practice-based music courses at the following institutions or
conservatoires:

- Birmingham Conservatoire
- Leeds College of Music
- Royal College of Music
- Royal Northern College of Music
- Royal Scottish Academy of Music and Drama
- Royal Welsh College of Music and Drama
- Trinity College of Music.

You may apply to up to six courses and to five courses via the UCAS
system as well, making a total of eleven in all. However, when you
have all your exam results and receive unconditional offers you
must decide between them and withdraw your application from
the other system.

CUKAS is administered by UCAS and your details will be held by
UCAS. The online application process is very like the UCAS one –
with its personal passwords and usernames. As with UCAS there is
also a **Track** service and the option of using **Extra**.

You will not, however, have the option of making the application in
Welsh. If you give the Royal Welsh College of Music and Drama as
one of your choices and you would like them to write to you in Welsh, you
may do this. CUKAS though, will only correspond with you in English.

Timing

You may apply from 2nd July – i.e. earlier than the UCAS date and all applications should be received by CUKAS by 1st October. This is much earlier than the UCAS deadline in January.

If you apply by this date you will be an 'on-time' applicant. After this date you will be a 'late' applicant. Auditions will commence on 15th October and conservatoires will make decisions on on-time applications by 5th January. You will need to reply to these by 31st January. If you apply after 1st February you will first have to contact conservatoires to see if any places are left You will be notified of auditions and offers of places by email.

CUKAS charges a £15 application fee regardless of the number of choices you make.

To start your application you will need to click on 'Log in' on the CUKAS homepage and then 'Apply for CUKAS courses'.

Once you are online you are required to complete the following sections:

- Welcome
- Generate an email verification code
- Verify your email address
- Further Details
- Education
- Qualifications
- Choices
- Referees
- Personal Statement
- View all.

Apply for CUKAS courses

There are Help notes at every point where you might need them but if you have a problem you can contact the CUKAS Customer Service Unit on 0871 468 0470 between 08:30 and 18:00, Monday to Friday.

The **Welcome** section gives you a personal ID. You will also be required to generate and then verify an email address before you can take your application any further. Working through the application is very like the procedure described already for UCAS. You can stop at any point, save the information and return to it later.

You will have to supply some information of a different kind however. For instance CUKAS wants to know your National Insurance Number. Why should they need this? The answer is that as a music student you might take part in performances for which you would receive payment. Concert organisers often need to have the National Insurance Number for each performer so they can pay them. A space is provided for you to give this in the **Further Details** section. Most of the questions in this section are similar to those on the UCAS application. Another additional requirement here this that you give the name of someone who can be contacted in case of an emergency during audition.

Education
Again, this is like the UCAS section of the same name. You have to give details of secondary schools attended and also details of any junior academies you have attended at any of the conservatoires.

Qualifications
Those required are ones you already hold and ones you are working towards.

Choices
You can choose up to six courses here. You will need to list the conservatoire and course codes, plus:

- your Study Type (one instrument or two) and in the case of two, give the main and second instruments – or two joint main ones and
- your Audition Method (whether you will attend at the conservatoire or at a designated overseas location or will be sending a recording or video). The latter option is for overseas applicants only.

Referees
Unlike the standard UCAS application this one requires two references. One must be from someone who can comment on your academic ability the other on

your practical music skills and commitment to a career in music. Normally this would be your principal study teacher or head of music.

You will now have to revert to old fashioned snail mail. You need to supply your referees with copies of the reference form in this section, either by post or email AND with a stamped addressed envelope for *each* conservatoire that you are applying to. This is because they must personally sign the reference form. This means that if you have used all six choices you will need 12 forms. (Full instructions on what to do are given here.)

Personal Statement

This gives you the chance to stand out and sell yourself to the admissions staff. See Chapter 5 for advice on how to complete this part of the application.

View all

Here you can look at all the information you have given. Check it carefully and submit it. It is advisable to print off and keep a paper copy of the application so that you can have it in front of you if you need to contact either CUKAS or a conservatoire about any points.

CUKAS Timetable

DATE	EVENT
2nd July	Opening date for applications.
1st October	Closing date for 'on time' applications.
2nd October	Opening date for 'late' applications.
15th October	Auditions begin.
31st January	Applicants must reply to offers if CUKAS received decisions for all their choices by 5th January.
31st March	Applicants must reply to offers if CUKAS received decisions for all their choices by 5th March.
31st July	Applicants must reply to offers if CUKAS received decisions for all their choices by 15th July.

25th August	Applicants must reply to offers if CUKAS received decisions for all their choices by 8th August.
30th September	Applicants must reply to offers if CUKAS received decisions for all their choices after 8th August.

Remember that if, when you have all your exam results, you are offered confirmed places in both the UCAS and CUKAS systems you must choose one course only and withdraw from the other system.

Some highly regarded conservatoires, notably the Royal Academy of Music and the Guildhall School of Music, are outside the CUKAS system. You need to apply to any conservatoires not listed under CUKAS above by obtaining individual application forms (from their websites).

It is worth noting that competition to all the UK conservatoires is fierce since they attract applicants from all over the world. This is particularly so in London. Looking at application statistics is rather misleading since they show competition for places at the rate of only six to ten applicants per place (you might have expected 30 or 40). It's a bit like Oxford and Cambridge – where only outstanding students apply. You will need high instrumental grades – possibly grade 7 but 8 would be realistic, plus excellent references from instrument teachers. That is to get to the audition – on which much depends since conservatoires are looking to judge potential as well as achievement.

USEFUL SOURCES OF INFORMATION

Books
Trotman Publishing in association with UCAS. *How to Complete Your UCAS Application*, Trotman Publishing, 2008.

Telephone numbers
CUKAS Customer Service Helpline
0871 468 0470, Monday to Friday, 08.30–18.00.

UCAS Customer Service Helpline
0871 468 0468, Monday to Friday, 08.30–18.00.

CHAPTER THREE
CHOOSING YOUR COURSE AND INSTITUTION

So, you are thinking about what to study and where to do so. Which comes first the course or the place? And when you are making your choices how do you find accurate information to help you compare different places? This was touched on in the Introduction and will be covered more fully later in this chapter.

It's easy for some people. They have always wanted to be a vet or an actor or have a passion for literature or the environment. But a lot of people simply don't know how to choose a subject at first, let alone where to do it.

Your first decision really must be the course/subject/programme. (Different HEIs have different titles.) OK, so there are some people who say 'I'm going to University X and that's the most important thing. It doesn't matter which subject I do.' Some even choose a university and then play tactics – looking for the course with the lowest entry requirements. It can work. But it doesn't do so very often. It doesn't work for two reasons. First, you have to get past the admissions tutor who is looking for evidence of enthusiasm for a subject and commitment to studying it (more on this in Chapters 4, 5 and 7). Second, even if you manage to bluff your way in you are going to be faced with study of this subject for three or four years. You have to like a subject much more than you do even for A or Higher level, where it is one of three or four subjects. At degree level you will concentrate on one subject or area. It follows that the work will be much deeper and intensive. Three years spent on something that barely interests you? No. That way leads to dropping out.

Choosing the right course then is very important. It's also very difficult! There is so much advice and information out there that you can suffer from overload. There are over 50,000 different degree subjects that you can study. Obviously that number reduces immediately as you have to have the right school subjects behind you as a base for applying. Still, this doesn't mean that you have to spend an entire year before you apply drowning in a sea of paper or spending 23 hours a day wading through websites. For a start you may well have a clear idea of what you want to study or be hesitating between one, two or three. When you have finally decided which one it is to be you can start to look at resources, like the UCAS website, books in your school or college library that offer advice on applications, and then you can begin to make a shortlist.

Does it matter if you haven't decided on a career yet? No. Not many people have at this stage. And around 40% of jobs advertised for graduates are open to students from any subject. When I was looking for case studies to include in a book *What Can I do with an Arts Degree?* I was able to include an English graduate working as a web consultant, a philosophy graduate in publishing, a classics graduate in human resources, a modern languages graduate in management consultancy and a historian in investment banking (among many other examples). On the other hand it's not a good plan to do a degree in languages and then decide that you would rather be a brain surgeon. Thinking about possible careers *would* be useful. And if you have no ideas now, talk to your university or college careers service staff in your first or second year.

When you have chosen a subject you then have to decide how much you want to specialise within it. It's very different from A or Higher level where what you study is predetermined. Take geography for instance – 65 HEIs offer courses in single subject geography. Many offer combined courses too. And apart from the obvious options of human or physical geography there are courses in environmental, regional, social and urban geography to name but a few. When it comes to history, 85 HEIs offer it as a single subject and there are 37 different specialist courses, such as business, church, maritime or political history.

You have a number of alternatives when considering what kind of course would suit you. Will you for instance continue with your **favourite subject**? Bearing mind the different specialisms that could be on offer, think about what aspects of your subject you enjoy studying now, as you could focus on these on your course.

Or what about a **new one**? There are dozens of subjects you can start from scratch at university – from agriculture to water sports management. The opportunity to try something different may be just what you want, but do check just what the subject involves before applying or you may end up disappointed!

Combined courses appeal to a lot of people. You may have a strong interest in more than one subject. For example, you may wish to pursue an interest in business studies whilst learning Spanish. Do a search and you will easily find courses that combine the two, many of which offer Spanish at beginners' level. A combined or joint course provides a good way to sample something new while keeping the safety factor of sticking with a known subject. There are various ways of mixing and matching the subjects – equal study of both or a major/minor combination of subjects which means you can devote more time to one of them. 'But is a two subject degree as good a single one?' I hear you ask. If you were thinking of an academic career then yes, one would be better. But apart from research, there are few careers that require an in-depth specialist knowledge of one subject.

Then there are **sandwich courses**. They involve blocks of full-time study followed by periods of work experience. A 'thick' sandwich usually involves a year out; a 'thin' sandwich involves two periods of six months. This does lengthen the course, but also allows you to obtain practical experience in the real world – a definite plus when you start to job hunt towards the end of your course.

Whichever type of course you choose its content is important. You need to examine this very closely. Two courses with the same title can be very different at different HEIs. A good example of this is the area of modern languages. Some courses concentrate on language skills while others bring in study of the culture, history and literature of the countries in which the languages are spoken. It's also useful to look at the content of each year of the course. You might find that the first year topics are interesting but ones studied later on less so.

Is that enough to think about? No! Another very important point to research is an HEI's teaching and assessment methods. Students react differently to different ways of learning and different ways of assessing their work. This is especially true in higher education where you are likely to come across a wide variety of both forms of assessment and teaching methods. The way your work is assessed could make all the difference to whether you pass or fail. Some people do best under exam pressure, others hate it. You might be a steady worker or

SUMMARY: TYPES OF COURSE

Full Time Academic Degree
This usually lasts three years full-time. Some, for example modern language courses, take four years and include a year abroad.

Full Time Vocational Degree
As they include work experience and partial training for a particular job, vocational courses last longer e.g. architecture, engineering, medicine and occupational therapy. They often need to be followed by more professional training to lead to the full qualification.

Sandwich Degree
They include up to 12 months' industrial experience, so again courses are longer – usually four years. Examples include business studies, computing and engineering.

Foundation Degree
This is a vocational course with work experience and has strong links with employers. It normally takes two years. It can be followed by two more years to convert into a full degree or can lead to employment. Work experience is included. Courses are available in a very wide range of subjects.

Higher National Diploma
This takes two years full time but some longer sandwich courses are available. Like the Foundation degree (which is gradually replacing the HND) it is vocational and has strong links with employers. Work experience is included. Many students convert the Diploma to a degree through further study.

a last-minute crammer. Any combination of the following assessment methods may be used – yearly examinations, continuous assessment, modular exams, project, dissertation or extended essay, final examinations. It is quite rare now for a final exam at the end of the course to be the only assessment tool.

WHERE?

When you have chosen a subject where are you going to do it? Do you want:

- A campus university?
- A city centre site?

- A small place?
- Somewhere that can enable you to carry on with a particular extra-curricular interest, for example a particular sport or sailing (no Midlands city then)? Most HEIs have a large number of clubs and societies so you could easily check this.
- Somewhere with a good reputation? A tricky one, this. See **League Tables.**

Home or away?

How far from home do you want to be? Near enough to make several visits each term to see parents, boy/girl friend? Further away because you want to be independent? Or will you live at home as an increasing number of students do?

Living at home as its advantages – the main one being financial. You might miss out a bit on social life or hall parties, but if the late night transport system is good, this needn't be the case. If you decide to move away, and most students still do, you'll need to decide between catered and self-catering accommodation. Can you cook? Are you gregarious or a loner?

Most people use varying combinations of these factors when choosing where to apply.

Narrowing the choice

A good place to start is the UCAS website. You can start by reading the general articles on course and subject choice and on life as a higher education student. More detail comes in the form of the alphabetical list of subjects. Click on to one of these and you will find some very useful condensed information in the form of **Entry Profiles**. Each HEI has been asked to list information about the course you are looking at, plus some information on the HEI itself. You can then follow the link to the HEI's website.

The information in the **Entry Profiles** sections comes in question and answer format. They are not standard though. Some entries are better than others! Depending on which HEI you are checking you mind find any of the following topics covered:

- What can this course offer me?
- Is this the right course for me?

- What are the entry requirements?
- What does the programme cover?
- What are the special features of this programme?
- What study facilities are available?
- What do current and past students say about the programme?
- What flexibility is there with this programme?
- What are the career opportunities?
- Do you have the following skills?
- Would you like the opportunity to develop these skills?

There might be sections on:

- About this institution
- Open Days, tours and visits
- Interviews – whether the department uses interviews as part of the selection procedure
- Admission statistics
- Tips on application
- Fees, bursaries and financial support.

The above examples are all taken from different HEIs' **Entry Profiles**.

Then you can move on to more detailed research. There are all kinds of sources of information on different HEIs. You could and might choose any of the following:

- HEI websites – They hold a lot of information and most of you will head for them fairly early on in your search. You can pick some at random, make a shortlist of places based on the area/region you would like to study in. You can use sources like the student section of the UCAS website to help you narrow down your choice.
- HEI prospectuses – which you can find in school or college, in local libraries and increasingly of course, on the internet. I would suggest browsing on line then asking for copies of ones that attract you to be sent to you as hard copy. It's much easier to compare and contrast details when you have a few of them in front of you. You don't need to store masses of them. Make a shortlist first.

■ Family, friends, people you know who have studied at particular HEIs recently – 'Recently' is the key. You don't want out-of-date information. Try and talk to people who have been to, or are currently at, the HEIs that you are considering. This can give you a valuable insight into what the social life, accommodation, sporting facilities and teaching methods are really like. Check where past students of your school or college have gone and get in touch with them. Is there a list available for you to consult?

■ Open Days – These are easily the best means of checking out an HEI and are good for getting a real feel of what a university or college is like. Don't forget to look at the town or city as well – it could be your home for the next three or four years.

Points to check:

■ Accommodation – What arrangements are available for first years? Are you guaranteed accommodation? What are university halls like? Do they provide meals? How much does it cost?

■ Departmental facilities – Are they up-to-date? Do they have the latest equipment? What teaching and assessment methods do they use?

■ Other academic study facilities – What are the library and computing facilities like?

■ Social and sporting facilities – What does the Students' Union provide? Does the sports centre look good? What clubs and societies are there?

■ General impressions of the site – Does it look a nice place, and at the end of the day would you want to live there?

HOW SOME STUDENTS CHOSE THEIR COURSES

MATTHEW, STUDYING PHYSICS AT OXFORD

'When it came to choosing universities I wanted to apply to some of the best ones for Physics. I discussed the choice with teachers and with my father, who is a physics graduate. I also went by common perceptions of which are the best universities for the subject and looked at some of the subject league tables. I think that it is important to look at these rather than the overall ones because sometimes the best universities may not be so good in a particular subject. My final choice was Oxford, Bath, Bristol, Lancaster, Southampton and Warwick. (Until this year students were allowed six choices.)

'I visited Bath, Bristol and Warwick, some of them twice, and I went to Open Days at two Oxford colleges in addition to the general Oxford one. I think that some people don't know about these but I would definitely advise going. They were both worthwhile.'

ANNA, STUDYING MEDICINE AT DURHAM

'When I decided on Medicine I was faced with the fact that I had only a limited number of places to apply to because I hadn't chosen to do A level Chemistry. I decided to drop General Studies and take AS Chemistry plus Science for Public Understanding in my second year along with my three A2 subjects. It was hard work but it was worth it. My college careers adviser helped me to choose medical schools that did not require A level Chemistry. I finally applied to Durham and Newcastle (which jointly run a medical school), the University of East Anglia and Sheffield. You can apply to Newcastle and Durham as one application and leave the two universities to allocate you to one campus or apply to both separately. I applied to both.'

CHETAN HAS APPLIED TO DO AUTOMOTIVE ENGINEERING

'During his AS year Chetan was in a real career dilemma. He came from a medical family – 'My father and sister are doctors' – but he also loved cars. Medicine, he felt he knew about and would be a safe choice. Automotive Engineering would be new. He had a lot of support from his family – 'They just wanted me to be happy and successful in whatever I chose to do. There was no pressure to enter medicine', and from his careers adviser. The dilemma continued however, until his careers adviser was contacted by Channel 4 TV and asked to recommend students in Chetan's position to take part in a programme Vocation, Vocation, Vocation. Between January and September 2007 Chetan was exposed to a variety of experiences and was filmed for the programme. 'I visited automotive companies, met lecturers and professors on top courses and spent some time doing voluntary work in a hospice.' Finally, Automotive Engineering won.

'The knowledge and understanding that Chetan gained impressed admissions staff at Loughborough University so much that he was made an immediate offer. 'I was able to draw on my experiences when writing my personal statement and explain how I was convinced that this was the course for me. I received a letter saying that they were going to make me an offer but wanted me to come on a visit first and have an interview during the course of it. The interview only lasted about two minutes! The interviewers had seen the programmes, and knew all about me and how I had reached my career decision.' He now has to get ABB or AAC with a minimum of grade B in Maths and grade C in Physics in order to take up the place.'

ADAM IS A FINAL YEAR DRAMA STUDENT

'Adam made a shortlist of ten drama courses, choosing ones that were members of the Conference of Drama Schools and choosing vocational acting courses as opposed to academic degrees. He soon realised that he must limit his number of applications due to the time and money he would have to spend on audition fees and travelling to them. In the end he applied to three. Bristol rejected him after the first round audition. He also progressed no further than the first round at RADA. The Guildford School of Acting recalled and subsequently accepted Adam on to the three year BA course.'

And now to:

LEAGUE TABLES

❝ I wish we had just one set of league tables that use the criteria that we as students would like to use.❞
AMIR, A CAMBRIDGE APPLICANT.

'Also, the present ones are not perfect. They contradict each other so much! I found that Portsmouth University came second in one and in another it wasn't even in the top 50'. Amir also spotted the fact that positions change from year to year. 'I looked at library copies and then, on advice from teachers, went online to find the most up-to-date data. In a lot of cases it was different in different surveys!'

How do league tables work?

They use various sets of data, obtained from different sources and given different weightings, to place HEIs in rank order. The first thing that many students and parents – not to mention some teachers and careers advisers – ask is a very straightforward question i.e. 'Which are the best universities?' and go straight to the rank order of the universities that have been measured. Unfortunately, there is no simple answer. The scores used to create the rank orders can often be very different in different league tables for the same university, as Amir (above) found. League tables do contain some useful information *if you know how to use them*.

A quick look at some of the criteria used in each league table shows that HEIs are quite different. What you do see though is that the top five or so have the same or similar rankings in all the tables.

So how do they arrive at their conclusions?

Newspapers usually base their tables on data published by the Higher Education Statistics Agency (HESA), but they use it in different ways. Nearly always they look at entry requirements, staff/student ratio, and employment rates but some factors are included because they are likely to appeal to the individual newspaper's readership. *The Times*, for instance example, stresses research and staffing levels more than *The Guardian* does. Another common indicator used is the result of The Research Assessment Exercise (RAE) which is conducted jointly by the Higher Education Funding Council for England, the Scottish Funding Council, the Higher Education Funding Council for Wales and the Department for Employment and Learning, Northern Ireland. The purpose of the RAE is to rate the quality of research done in HEIs. The results are then used in determining the amount of research grants they will receive from the funding bodies.

League tables are contentious. Many universities criticise them for all sorts of reasons. Some are those given above. Others include the unreliability of some data, the sampling methods, the different weightings given to the criteria used and the fact that smaller specialist HEIs often appear at a disadvantage. Some also make the point that there may be very little difference in the scores of HEIs clustered together in the top or middle rankings. Nevertheless you will see in prospectuses and on websites that they can be quick to mention a favourable rating when they have received one!

UCAS does not produce any league tables of its own – and on its websites for both students and parents lists all the caveats about checking the criteria used and assessing whether they are the correct ones for you. It does however, say 'For information and impartial advice check the *Times Online* or *The Good University Guide* (an interactive site which allows you to alter the weightings of the different measures to suit your own requirements and so create your own unique table). UCAS also supports *Unistats* which is owned by the Higher Education Funding Council for England where Unistasts is concerned, it also acts on behalf of the Higher Education Funding Council for Wales, the Department for Employment and Learning Northern Ireland and the Scottish Funding Council.

Two particular caveats of my own. Staff student ratio? What does that actually mean? Does it mean that every member of staff is actively involved in teaching students and that classes are therefore smaller? Or are some eminent staff members always travelling to present papers at lectures all over the world? Do many concentrate on teaching postgraduates? Or on their own research? Employment rates. Do the figures refer to data collected within a few months of graduation when most former students are employed – but many will be in temporary jobs while they work out their next step or pay off their debts? Or does the figure refer to those who are in jobs that genuinely require their degree level skills?

The different tables

The Times Good University Guide 2008

These tables use the following criteria:

- Student Satisfaction
- Research Assessment
- Entry Standards
- Staff-Student Ratio
- Spending on Libraries and Computers
- Spend on Facilities
- The Number of Good Honours Degrees Awarded
- Graduate Prospects
- Completion Rates.

Looking at it you would see straight away that Oxford in first place scores heavily on all these factors with Cambridge, Imperial, the LSE and University

College, London not far behind. Lower down the tables however, you will find Leicester, Reading and Royal Holloway, London coming higher on overall ratings than the Russell Group Universities Birmingham, Cardiff and Manchester. Look at some of the individual criteria ratings though and you get a different picture.

Sources for this survey include the National Student Survey, the 2001 Research Assessment Exercise (the next one is due out very soon) and HESA.

If you use the online version you can use tick boxes to compare two or more HEIs and compile your own shortlist.

The Guardian University Guide 2008

The Guardian's University Guide 2008 is aimed at helping prospective students choose courses, so it concentrates less than alternative tables on research ratings. It judges courses on the student verdict on teaching and feedback, gathered from final year undergraduates in the National Student Survey, plus spending per student, staff/student ratios, job prospects, entry qualifications and a value-added measure comparing individuals' entry qualifications with their degree results.' (Statement from *The Guardian's* website.)

The following criteria are used here:

- Teaching
- Feedback
- Spend Per Student
- Staff-Student Ratio
- Job Prospects
- Value Added
- Entry.

If you use the online version (which has some corrections that do not appear in the book) you can use drop down lists to compare different HEIs and subjects.

The Good University Guide

The *Good University Guide* site is managed by Constable and Robinson in collaboration with Mayfield University Consultants and The University of Sheffield. This one allows you to work on it interactively and create your own ranking and there is also a select and compare feature. You may not choose your own criteria to use, but you may change the priority given to them in the original tables.

The criteria used are:

- Research Assessment
- Student-Staff Ratio
- Academic Services Spend
- Facilities Spend
- Good Honours Degrees
- Graduate Prospects
- Entry Standards.

Information sources include HESA, the 2001 Research Assessment Exercise and the National Student Survey.

Once again you will see universities in different rank order – and again you will find some that appear in all/none/some of the three tables used as examples so far.

If you want to customise the tables for your own purposes you can do so on this website. The weightings given to the different criteria are 1.5 for Student Satisfaction and Research Assessment with 1.00 for all the others. By using the tabs offered to you, you can weight these factors anywhere from 0 to 2.5.

The Times Higher Education Supplement – QS Top Universities World University Rankings

The Times Higher Education Supplement – QS Top Universities World University Rankings is now in its fourth year of publication. It lists the top 200 universities in the world – and finds that the majority are in the USA, followed by the UK. The only other countries to appear in the top 20 are Australia, Canada, Hong Kong and Japan.

These tables are designed not just for prospective first degree students but also, or even more so, for graduates looking for research places and university staff looking for jobs in their field throughout the world. It can be interesting to see how our HEIs compare with others globally.

Quacquarelli Symonds, an 'international provider of career and educational information' is one half of the partnership and collects the data. The criteria the company uses are: Peer Review Score (in other words, universities vote for each other), Employer Review Score, Staff/Student Score, Citations Staff Score, International Staff Score and International Student Score. These individual scores are then combined to produce the overall rankings. The people questioned in the surveys are just over 5,100 active academics in universities across the world, who are asked to list up to 30 universities they regard as leaders in the academic field (with restrictions on voting for one's own university in place!) and recruiters of graduates – nearly 1,500 major global and national employers who are asked which universities they like to hire from. Also taken into account are the percentages of international staff and students each institution is able to attract and the number of citations of published research (that means the number of times papers produced in one university are quoted by people working in others).

In addition to an overall table there are league tables for individual subject areas – arts and humanities, life sciences and biomedicine, natural sciences, social sciences and technology. You can also look under other individual criteria, namely Top Ten Peer Review, Top Ten Employer Review, Top Ten International Staff, Top Ten Staff-Student Ratio, Top Ten International Students and Top Ten Citations for Staff Members.

THE TOP 20 BRITISH UNIVERSITIES ACCORDING TO DIFFERENT LEAGUE TABLES

The Times Good University Guide 2008
(www.timesonline.co.uk/gug)
Top 20 universities for 2007 are shown in brackets. (Showing that positions can and do change from year to year.)

1.	Oxford (Oxford)
2.	Cambridge (Cambridge)
3.	Imperial College, London (Imperial)
4.	LSE (LSE)
5.	St Andrews (UCL)
6.	UCL (Loughborough)
7.	Warwick (Bristol)
8.	Bristol (Warwick)
9.	Durham (Bath)
10.	King's Collogo, London (Durham)
11.	Bath (Edinburgh)
12.	Loughborough (Royal Holloway)
13.	Edinburgh (Aston)
14.	Southampton (Nottingham)
15.	Aston (York)
16.	York (Cardiff)
17.	Exeter (King's College, London)
18.	School of Oriental and African Studies, London
19.	Nottingham
20.	University of East Anglia.

In 2007 Leicester, SOAS and St Andrews and were in joint 18th place.

The Guardian University Guide 2008
(www.educationguardian.co.uk/universityguide2008)

1.	Oxford
2.	Cambridge
3.	Imperial College, London
4.	St Andrews
5.	UCL
6.	LSE
7.	Edinburgh
8.	Warwick
9.	Loughborough

	Bath
	SOAS
	King's College, London
	Southampton
	Bristol
	York
16	Manchester
	Durham
	Birmingham
	Nottingham
	Leeds.

The Good University Guide 2008

(www.thegooduniversityguide.org.uk)

	Cambridge
	Oxford
	Imperial College, London
	LSE
	St Andrews
	UCL
	Bristol
	Warwick
	Bath
	Durham
	Loughborough
	Aston
	Royal Holloway
	Nottingham and York
	Edinburgh
	Exeter and King's College, London
	Lancaster
	East Anglia, Leicester and Southampton.

The Times Higher Education Supplement – QS Top Universities
(www.timeshighereducation.co.uk)

1.	Cambridge
2.	Oxford
3.	Imperial
4.	UCL
5.	Edinburgh
6.	King's College, London
7.	Manchester
8.	Bristol
9.	Warwick
10.	LSE
11.	Birmingham
12.	Sheffield
13.	Nottingham
14.	York
15.	St Andrews
16.	Leeds
17.	Southampton
18.	Glasgow
19.	Cardiff
20.	Liverpool.

I have extracted the above list from *The Times Higher Education Supplement – QS listings* which were compiled in November 2007 and which give the top 200 universities *in the world*. Only four of our universities make it into the top 20, consisting of:

1.	Harvard	USA
2=	**Cambridge**	**UK**
2=	**Oxford**	**UK**
2=	Yale	USA
5.	**Imperial College, London**	**UK**

6	Princeton	USA
	California Institute of Technology	USA
=	Chicago	USA
9	**University College, London**	**UK**
0	Massachusetts Institute of Technology	USA
1	Columbia	USA
2	McGill	Canada
3	Duke	USA
4	Pennsylvania	USA
5	Johns Hopkins	USA
6	Australian National University	Australia
7	Tokyo	Japan
8.	Hong Kong	Hong Kong
9	Stanford	USA
20=	Carnegie Mellon	USA
20=	Cornell	USA

Oxford and Imperial College, London had different rankings in 2006, and in that year University College, London did not make it into the top 20 – at position 25. The London School of Economics in the same year was rated 17th.

SUBJECT LEAGUE TABLES

❛ I think that it is important to look at these rather than the overall ones because sometimes the best universities may not be so good in a particular subject.❜
MATTHEW, CURRENT OXFORD STUDENT.

You have now seen how easy it is to get different results for overall ranking of HEIs by using different league tables. The same applies to subject league tables! You can use all the league tables quoted to draw up lists ratings different subjects. The least useful of these is *The Times Higher Education Supplement – QS* one since it covers broad areas of study only whereas the others report on individual subjects.

The same warnings apply and I am not going to go into much further detail but leave you to consult the websites or books for yourself. But looking for an example I did a search on geography and here is the result. **N.B.** *Top Universities* puts geography on its own. The other two combine it with environmental science/studies.

The Times Good University Guide 2008

1.	Cambridge
2.	LSE
3.	Durham
4	Bristol
5.	UCL
6.	Oxford
7.	Edinburgh
8.	Southampton
9.	Nottingham
10.	Sheffield
11.	Aberdeen
12.	Newcastle
13.	Royal Holloway
14=	Cardiff
14=	Leeds
16.	King's College, London
17.	St Andrews
18.	Reading
10.	East Anglia
20.	Loughborough.

The Guardian University Guide 2008

1.	Cambridge
2.	Oxford
3.	Bristol
4.	UCL

5	Edinburgh
6	Durham
	LSE
8	Reading
9	Southampton
0	East Anglia
11	Bradford
2	St Andrews
3	Queen Mary, London
4	Aberystwyth
5	Staffordshire
6	Brunel
	Leicester
8	King's College, London
9	Nottingham
20	Hull.

The Good University Guide 2008
(www.thegooduniversityguide.org.uk)

	LSE
	Cambridge
	Durham
4	Bristol
	UCL
	Oxford
	Edinburgh
	Southampton
	Nottingham
0	Sheffield
1	Aberdeen
2	Newcastle
3	Leeds
4	Royal Holloway

15.	Cardiff
16=	King's College, London
16=	St Andrews
18.	Loughborough
19.	Reading
20.	East Anglia.

How some more students made their choices

ALEX, STUDYING TRANSPORTATION DESIGN AT NORTHUMBRIA UNIVERSITY

This is not a university that features in any 'top ten' or 'top twenty' lists but this particular course is one that has an excellent success rate for graduate employment. Recent graduates are working for Bentley, Drive, Ford, Hyundai, VW and Sealine (yacht manufacturer). This is a reminder that the best courses are not always in the universities that score highly *overall* in league tables!

'I have always been interested in cars but my main interest is in marine design. I have always spent part of my free time designing both boats and cars. I love the combination of creativity and technology. I researched universities very carefully. I didn't use league tables or anything like that. I went on advice from my teachers and my own evaluation of courses. I looked at university and departmental websites and I read prospectuses and course details. I narrowed my choice down to two. One of them took a large number of first year students and there was a rumour that they failed a lot of them at the end of the year. I decided not to apply there and to put all my effort into getting a place at Northumbria.

'I liked the situation of the university and its facilities (I live in the North East so it was an easy place to visit and look round). What really stood out for me was the fact there were such good links with employers. During the course I would be able to visit top companies in this country and abroad. They could organise third year placements with such companies. I reasoned that if they had such good links with companies like Lamborghini, Porsche, Maserati and VW Jaguar I would be likely to get a good placement, forge my own links and eventually get a good job. My plans at present actually are to do an MSc. then hopefully work for a yacht designer. I am also interested in some external design houses or some car builders that do one-off concept projects.'

STEPHEN HAS APPLIED TO DO ENVIRONMENTAL SCIENCE

'In May last year I went to a higher education fair. We got programmes in advance in school and could choose to attend three different talks on higher education courses before going to look at the university and college stands. It was like an exhibition with representatives from different places to answer questions and give you prospectuses. I got a few ideas on courses and collected a couple of prospectuses from the universities which appealed to me most at the time.

'I started my research on the UCAS website where I looked at a number of universities. Then I looked at their prospectuses and at the Entry Profiles section on the UCAS site. I also visited departments' websites to get all the detail I wanted - even down to a list of the modules I would be studying in the first, second and third years.

'I had an initial list of 12 universities. I got this list down to five with some help from my father who had already been through this process with my brother. He suggested that I should include some places whose grades were lower than the others' as a safety measure. To be honest however, I also wanted to go to a 'top' university and Nottingham which came high in league tables was my preferred choice.

'The last step was going to open days. There is no substitute for doing this. After I received all five offers I was very torn between which ones to choose as my firm and insurance offers so I went back Nottingham, which was one of them, and had a second look round - a very detailed one this time with a checklist of points to cover. Although it was my second visit to the University, I was undoubtedly more impressed this time round!'

LUCIE HAS APPLIED TO DO A PSYCHOLOGY DEGREE

'I got some preliminary ideas at a higher education fair. Representatives from a lot of universities were there and you could collect or order prospectuses. I then used some league tables, looking at one that placed the universities in rank order and a subject one that rated Psychology at different places. Open days came next - I attended five, and finally I went through all my prospectuses very carefully and made notes. I also used one of the alternative guides – The Virgin Alternative Guide to British Universities which gives you information from the student point of view. After that I felt that I had done all that I could and was ready to make a shortlist.'

RISHI HAS APPLIED TO DO AERONAUTICAL ENGINEERING

Rishi researched his choice of universities very thoroughly. He began by looking at some of the league tables and used both university and subject tables.

'I used the Times Good University Guide as a benchmark, and compared some of the others with its results. I then made a list and started to discuss it with other people. I found my careers adviser the most helpful. She really was a major influence in my choice but I also talked to former students from my school who were currently studying at the places I was interested in. I also researched through the individual universities' websites, whilst paying extra attention to what was offered in each course, not only by the university itself. My priorities lay not with the social aspects of the universities, but with their academic background. I didn't give accommodation the attention I should have done, looking back but, fortunately, I am very happy with what I have been offered.'

INFORMATION SOURCES

Books
The Big Guide 2008, UCAS
The UCAS Directory 2008
The Virgin Alternative Guide to British Universities, Virgin
Degree Course Offers 2008, Trotman
Choosing Your Degree Course and University, Trotman
Student Book 2008, Trotman

Websites
www.ucas.com
www.studentuk.com
www.hesa.ac.uk
www.thegooduniversityguide.org.uk

CHAPTER FOUR

MAXIMISING YOUR CHANCES

WHEN SHOULD YOU START THINKING ABOUT YOUR HIGHER EDUCATION APPLICATION?

As early as you can! You will have to apply about one year ahead of starting a higher education course – that is in the autumn term of Year 13. The various closing dates can creep up and take you by surprise.

It pays to get an application in early. If you do so you are more likely to receive decisions from HEIs early and can then choose between them and spend the rest of the year concentrating on exams rather than application forms and interviews.

ADAM HAS APPLIED FOR LAW

Adam got his degree course applications in early and received his first offer just one week later! The others came in good time too. He received the last one at the beginning of December and sent his final decision to UCAS in mid-February. He received offers from all five universities.

He says 'We were encouraged to start the process early. In my lower sixth year (year 12) I had a lot of help from the college careers department which organised information sessions and personal interviews. I also had a committed form teacher who saw us all individually towards the end of the autumn term. I started to do my own research in March and began to collect information and put some ideas together. In the summer term speakers from universities were invited in to talk to us and the college organised a visit to a higher education fair which was really helpful. During the summer I went to some Open Days.'

All the offers were sent without Adam attending any interviews. He would not have minded attending any since he was well prepared and had had practice runs at college. He did, however, visit all five universities after receiving the offers. Each *one offered an open day at which he could tour the campus, see accommodation facilities, listen to talks on studying his subjects and meet current students.*

Before you can complete an application you need to make an informed choice of course and you need to do the best you can to make your application stand out. How? By getting as much information as you can and by getting relevant experience where appropriate. HEI staff who select students for top courses can afford to be choosy. They will go for top exam grades *plus* other skills, aptitudes and experiences.

You should begin work on boosting your application in Year 12 – or even better earlier still.

WHAT SHOULD YOU BE DOING IN THE YEARS BEFORE TO MAXIMISE YOUR CHANCES OF GETTING ON TO A TOP COURSE?

Be informed

Find out as much as possible about higher education courses and the HEIs that offer them.

- Read prospectuses and course leaflets.
- Visit HEI websites.
- Ask other people for information – teachers, friends, students from your school or college who are now in higher education.
- Make some visits.
- Use your school or college's resources.

If you want to start getting advance information and are in an 11–16 school you might be able to visit the library in the nearest sixth-form college.

Higher education fairs

Many schools and colleges take coach loads of students to these. They are held at different times of year so you need to keep an eye open for advertisements. If you are in Year 11 and would like to go to one you could go on your own, with a group of friends or with your parents. Fairs are held in big exhibition halls where representatives from different HEIs have stands. There is usually a UCAS stand too.

Some fairs include presentations on general topics such as *Application*, *Finance* and *Student Life* that you can sign up for.

Open Days

These are often held in the summer term, and again there is no reason why you should not go to one if you are still in Year 11. They are major events at which HEIs show off their facilities, equipment, accommodation and environment. Again, you can attend presentations, this time on general topics but also on specific subjects. There are often separate sessions for parents on money matters.

LUCIE HAS APPLIED TO STUDY PSYCHOLOGY
She says that it is very important to attend Open Days.

'You get to see the campus and get a gut feeling about the place. Only you know where you will be happy. One or two of my friends for instance were put off some places when they visited the accommodation and thought that the rooms were too small. I found that I based my opinions on some of the subject talks I attended. If they were interesting I was inspired to find out more about the course. If not, I was put off by the thought of having to attend dull lectures!

'Most of the Open Days had the same format - campus tours, presentations on individual subjects, visits to accommodation and some general talks on things like application procedures and finance. I particularly appreciated the opportunity to visit Psychology departments and see the labs and other facilities. Most places have current students acting as guides and answering questions. Talking to them is really useful. You feel that you can ask questions that you would not ask the staff. I found that they gave very frank answers. For example, at one place I was told 'There is not much night life here but we make the best of it.'

If you attend some fairs and Open Days you are well on the way to having something concrete to put on your personal statement when the time comes. You will be able to write that you visited a particular faculty or department and asked for advice from staff there.

STEPHEN HAS APPLIED TO DO ENVIRONMENTAL SCIENCE
'Open Days give you the opportunity to attend a talk on the subject you are thinking about and to see the department and its facilities. You also get

tours of the campus or the different sites and if you are lucky, the town as well.

'At Plymouth we had a welcome talk in a large group, followed by presentations on accommodation and finance before splitting into smaller groups for campus tours. The lecturer who did the subject talk was amazing. I have never seen anyone more passionate about his subject or so keen to get students involved in helping the environment. I learned that the course emphasised fieldwork and encouraged students to go out and do things rather than sit in lectures.

'Portsmouth was another type of Open Day. It was run by the department and included a short interview. We were taken on a tour of the department and the university site, had lunch with some current students who could answer all our questions and were also given a tour of Portsmouth by minibus. During the day everyone had a one to one interview. Mine lasted about ten minutes and was not very formal. I was asked the standard questions - why I wanted to do Environmental Science, why I wanted to do it there and why I thought I was a suitable candidate!'

Taster courses

❝ By attending Headstart Insight into Engineering at Salford University, I received the opportunity to speak to other women that were successful in this field and also visited Arup in Manchester for a day.❞

DIVYA, ENGINEERING APPLICANT

One way to convince admissions tutors that you really know your stuff is to attend a taster course. These are held up and down the country, usually in school holidays, and last for anything from one to several days. Some are designed to show you what in depth study of your favourite subject would be like at degree level. Others are designed to introduce a new subject to you. Simulations, presentations, discussions, group exercises normally feature as does hands-on experience where possible. There is often the chance to talk to undergraduate students and professionals in particular careers.

There is often a cost involved in attending these courses. Some are run by commercial organisations and charge a fee. Others are provided by university departments and are free. Even if they do not make a charge there is still the cost of travel to think about. If finding the money would be a problem you should ask whether your school or college can provide any financial assistance.

Be prepared

If you are going to apply for a course in art and design for example, you will need to take a portfolio of work with you to interviews. Tutors like to see how students' work has developed over several years so it is worth choosing some of your best GCSE work and keeping it in a safe place. They also like to see work that they have done in their own time and is not influenced by teachers. It is therefore a very good idea to start a collection of pieces with notebooks explaining what you were aiming for in each one. This too can be started in Year 11

There is no rigid format for a portfolio but there are some guidelines. Admissions tutors want to see a broad variety of work – drawing, painting from observation, 3D work and if possible, computer-generated work and photography. An expensive folder is not essential but its presentation is important. Work should be put in either a logical or chronological order.

You may be expected at an interview to present your portfolio to one or two tutors and talk about it. You need your best work in it, and pieces that you are happy to talk about. You won't have any way of knowing which ones you might be asked about so it is not a good idea to have to include 'fillers'.

If you start work on the portfolio in plenty of time you will be well prepared with examples of your best work to choose from.

ALEX IS STUDYING TRANSPORTATION DESIGN AT NORTHUMBRIA UNIVERSITY. HE DID NOT HOWEVER, GO THERE STRAIGHT FROM SCHOOL

'On the advice of my art teacher I decided to an Art Foundation Course first. The reason for this was that we felt I needed to improve my design skills. My A level course had taught me to draw from life and still life but I had not done anything exciting or much on perspective. I did consider applying for direct entry and saw that I would need to obtain 180 UCAS points. However the entry requirements also stated "balanced portfolio"…

'That decision was a good one. The Foundation Course definitely helped me to develop the further skills I needed. In the first term we did two week rotations, with projects in different fields. After Christmas we specialised and I was advised to do so in 3D Design. I was able to work on modelling, sculpture and provide evidence of perspective. My tutor gave me a lot of guidance on preparing a portfolio of work geared towards the course at Northumbria. She also told me not to jettison my school work but to include examples of that too. They would want to see my drawing skills and also see the way in which my work had developed.

'So I prepared my portfolio carefully. I put pieces of work from GCSE, A level and Foundation Course work, and some work I had done in my own time, in chronological order and in sections with a written introduction to each one, explaining what was in there and how I had produced the pieces. Each section had a header page with two paragraphs and I annotated different pieces. It was not a particularly smart portfolio - a standard A2 size one, black with plastic sleeves inside.'

If you are going to apply for a vocational course you have to convince admissions staff of your knowledge and suitability for a particular profession. This is where work experience comes in.

Work experience and shadowing

Work experience organised by your school in Years 10 or 11 may be helpful, but sometimes it is not relevant to what you decide to apply for later. Some forms of work experience are not even available to younger students. There is also often an issue with age. Some hospitals and GPs for instance require students to be over 16 before they will take them on. This can be a problem for some school students in Year 11 who may still be 15 when they are offered work experience at school.

If you can organise some more in Year 12 this will be very helpful when you come to write your application (see Chapter 5 for examples of how some students were able to draw on their work experience in support of their applications).

You may be more likely to find a work shadowing placement at this stage. What is the difference between work shadowing and work experience?

Experience is hands-on. You get the chance to do some relevant work or parts of projects. Shadowing means spending some time with a professional person, observing their work and asking questions. They should involve you where possible and take the time to explain what they are doing. Shadowing is an obvious choice for professions like law and medicine. Students can hardly be let loose in operating theatres or prosecute cases...

How would make the arrangements?

- Your careers adviser or teacher might do this for you.
- Or they might provide you with names and addresses to contact.
- You could write to companies/organisations/hospitals yourself.
- Ask everyone you know who works in the relevant field. Try friends and relatives, neighbours, your friends' parents and your parents' friends. Chase up any lead.

If you find the placement by yourself this is another plus point. You can put this on the application and demonstrate both your enthusiasm and your initiative!

DIVYA HAS APPLIED TO STUDY CIVIL ENGINEERING

She did two different work experience placements during Year 12; the first at the head office of the international engineering and construction group Costain, the second with Halcrow, an international engineering consultancy. She arranged both placements for herself, using information supplied by her careers adviser.

'I learned so much at both companies. At Costain I spent time in different departments. I saw how important IT support is to a company, learned how companies tender for business and I shadowed a health and safety officer. I also did some real work. Another work experience student and I and I were given a proposed project to evaluate and report on.

'At Halcrow I shadowed engineers in the drainage and sewerage department and did some parts of their work for them - nothing too technical - things like calculations and flow rates. For example a large project involved updating and expanding a city's sewerage system that is no longer adequate for present day demands. I calculated some of the flow rates. I also accompanied engineers on visits. One was to negotiate with a farmer who thought that a new main sewer line was going to be too near his buildings. That was interesting.

'I thought that it was really important to get some work experience - partly so that I was sure in my own mind that this was what I wanted to do and partly to convince universities that I had done my research. This is a new subject for me and it leads to one particular career. It is not like applying to do a familiar subject like maths and choosing a career later.'

Divya put the following sentence, based on her work experience, in her personal statement:

'While shadowing a Health and Safety Advisor I visited the various sites where Costain was working and was shown how important the company took their health and safety and also how important an issue it has become in recent years. By visiting a member of the public concerned about the company's actions I also got the chance to see how significant communication is in this industry.'

RISHI HAS APPLIED TO STUDY AERONAUTICAL ENGINEERING

He managed to organise some extremely relevant work experience which came about through his love of flying and his membership of the Air Cadets.

'I have been a member since I was 13. Last year my squadron put my name forward for a gliding scholarship. This meant that I went regularly to RAF Halton, which is near my home, to learn to fly a motor glider.

'Normally the training takes two to three months but my flying hours kept being prolonged due to bad visibility and high winds, so I was there for nearly a year. As a result I got to know the instructors very well and they invited me back to do advanced training in my summer holidays. This involved furthering my abilities in cross-wind landings, steep turns and engine failures. At the end of the training I was privileged to do five more solo flights, after which I earned my Gold Wings. I now spend every Saturday at Halton as a Flight Staff Cadet, helping with cadet activities and also continuing my training to become an instructor.'

Rishi's work experience enabled him to include the following sentences in his personal statement on his degree course application.

'My enthusiasm impressed staff at RAF Halton to such an extent that I was invited for Advanced Training, earning me Gold Wings, 6 Solos and a National Gliding Qualification. Now, a Flight Staff Cadet at 613 Volunteer Gliding School, I manage Cadets, Aircraft Operations and also continue to progress to a Category C Instructor status, through further instruction.'

His college also participated in an Engineering Education Scheme in which teams of students worked with companies.

'As a Project Leader, with the National Grid, my team worked on a real problem: The sagging of pylon conductors due to high temperatures and currents. Our success in finding a productive yet cheap solution was the result of refined team work and perseverance; documented in a professional project report.'

Voluntary work

This can be an equally impressive activity to include in an application. It shows something about you as a person – that you are ready to give up some of your free time to help other people. It can also provide evidence of communication skills or experience in dealing with different age groups.

If you might want a career involving work with children you could think about helping to run a Brownie or Cub group. Getting a community sports leader award could be helpful if you decide to apply for anything related to sport. There are more ideas in Chapter 5.

ANNA IS A FIRST YEAR MEDICAL STUDENT AT DURHAM UNIVERSITY
She was well-prepared and had several different kinds of relevant experience to discuss.

'I went to an Open Day on Occupational Therapy, did a week's work experience on a hospital ward, another placement in a pharmacy, another week in a centre run by MIND and a day in a GP surgery. I would have liked to spend longer there but it was difficult for the practice as they had to contact every patient who was due in that day and get their permission to have me present.

'I learned different things on each placement and gradually I realised that I wanted to be a doctor. I wasn't allowed to do very much on the hospital ward because I hadn't been taught any basic nursing skills but I developed a role for myself, did whatever needed to be done that I was capable of and spent a lot of time talking to the patients. I was allowed to observe several procedures too. One was a heart scan. We had just started to study the heart in Biology, so it tied in really well with my academic work, but I didn't know very much. When the doctor asked me how many valves there were I got the answer wrong (the patient laughed!).

'I got really good experience of work with people who had Parkinsons and Alzheimers through my MIND placement and I did think for a while of doing a Psychology degree. But I reasoned that I would still have to train for a career afterwards and that by doing Medicine I could always specialise in Psychiatry if I chose to later.

'I worked in a pharmacy for a week and enjoyed learning about the different drugs but I realised that I wanted a career with patient contact.'

Performing Arts

Should you decide to apply for a course in this area – where competition is intense – you need as much amateur experience as possible. So you could join a dramatic or operatic society, orchestra or choir. You will probably do all of these activities in school or college, but if you have the time try to get some outside experience too. Get as much experience as you can. Start now.

You might be lucky enough to have opportunities to work professionally but this is not always possible.

ADAM IS IN HIS FINAL YEAR OF A DEGREE COURSE, A BA IN ACTING AT THE GUILDFORD SCHOOL OF ACTING (GSA).
GSA offers training in Acting, Musical Theatre and Stage Management in 2009 GSA will have a purpose-built school on the campus of Surrey University and its students will be full members of the University.

Adam's first stage performance was at the age of nine when he took part in a Gang Show at the Nuffield Theatre in Southampton. He then joined Stagecoach and soon discovered that acting was his love. He stayed five years with

Stagecoach and subsequently moved on to the Nuffield Youth Theatre as one of its first members. Through both organisations he was able to gain a lot of experience and take part in professional performances in Southampton.

'When I was eleven I appeared in the Wizard of Oz and in every Christmas show at the Nuffield for the next seven years. As I grew older I began to be offered different parts. I played Boy in Waiting for Godot, was in the community chorus of Antigone, and the chorus in Hamlet.

'Being able to mix with professional actors in the green room before and after performances was a great opportunity. I gained a lot by talking to them. One thing I soon realised was how pleased they all were to be in work. I certainly had no illusions that I was choosing a secure profession.'

What really convinced Adam to go ahead was the encouragement he received after being directed in a monologue piece. He moved to a sixth-form college where he took A levels in Drama and Theatre Studies and Music Technology together with an AVCE (Advanced Vocational Certificate of Education – now an A level programme) in Performing Arts

Finally

Beware the Russell Group

This may be the most important advice of all. Unfortunately, if you are already in Year 12 it is too late! You need to choose your A level/Higher/ Diploma subjects with care. In January 2008, *The Sunday Times* ran an article stating that the University of Cambridge and the London School of Economics were recommending against certain 'soft' A level and International Baccalaureate (IB) subjects.

Their lead, the article claimed, would be copied by other Russell Group universities.

The Russell Group immediately issued a statement to the effect that it did not blacklist any subject. But many of their members had lists of subjects they did not regard as 'an effective preparation for their courses'. What this meant was that normally only one should be offered in a package of three A levels, along with two 'traditional' ones.

Dr Wendy Piatt, Director General of The Russell Group, speaking for all its members, said 'Russell Group universities are increasing and improving the information they provide for potential students about the qualifications and skills they need to be successful in pursuing their chosen course. They now offer clear recommendations on the **package** of A levels (or equivalent) which would give the candidate the best grounding for a particular course and which would be a less ideal **combination** of A levels.'

There is nothing new in this incidentally. For years I made it part of my homework to read through every single university's prospectus each year and make a list of any subjects it did not accept. I then compiled a master list and passed it to all my teaching colleagues. As always, the situation varied in different HEIs. Some were happy to accept two subjects from their list in a three subject combination while others preferred to see only one.

However, it appears that many schools and colleges are not aware of this distinction between subjects.

'Our institutions are now posting **Entry Profiles** on the UCAS website, giving detailed guidance to learners as early as Year 11 on how they might best tailor their post-16 study to their HE needs' said Dr Piatt.

The list of less acceptable subjects does vary. The LSE and Cambridge lists are not identical for instance. So you do need to look at the information in each university's **Entry Profile**. You may also need to contact universities you are considering applying to and asking whether certain subjects are accepted for a *particular course* as there may be exceptions if an otherwise non-recommended subject is particularly relevant to it.

However, these subjects are the ones on the Cambridge list – and many are likely to turn up on lists from other places. If you are considering taking more than one of them do your research!

- Accounting
- Art and Design
- Business Studies
- Communication Studies

- Dance
- Design and Technology
- Drama and Theatre Studies
- Film Studies
- Health and Social Care
- Home Economics
- Information and Communication Technology
- Leisure Studies
- Media Studies
- Music Technology
- Performance Studies
- Performing Arts
- Photography
- Physical Education
- Sports Studies.

Cambridge also states that Critical Thinking and General Studies will only be accepted as fourth A levels and will not therefore be included in a conditional offer.

The following IB subjects are also listed:

- Business and Management
- Design and Technology
- Information Technology in a Global Society
- Theatre Arts
- Visual Arts.

CHAPTER FIVE
WHAT ARE THEY LOOKING FOR?

 he top universities and courses are looking for specific qualities in their applicants and – given the ratio of applicants to places – they can afford to insist on them.

WHAT ARE THESE QUALITIES?

Academic grades are extremely important. Given a choice, most admissions tutors would probably prefer to receive applications from students who are predicted to get straight A grades (or equivalent). That way they know that the students will have no difficulty with the academic and theoretical parts of the course.

But, and it is a big but, exam grades are not everything. What admissions tutors really want, regardless of whether the course is academic or vocational, is real interest in a subject.

Time and time again the word *passion* crops up. *Or enthusiasm*. They want someone with a burning desire to study their subject. Some students can achieve top grades effortlessly, without being really interested in any subject. Admittedly though, good grades and interest in a subject do usually go together. So enthusiasm and interest go hand in hand with good grades and can even overtake them in admissions tutors' wish lists. A candidate brimming with enthusiasm may be more attractive and be given a chance with marginally lower grades than normally asked for. Admissions staff for vocational courses usually use the word *commitment* and look for evidence of students' motivation for choosing their course.

Then there is the fact that people with the highest academic qualifications could be people with nothing else outstanding to recommend them. They could have no interests outside exam work. This is not particularly healthy and could imply that they have to spend all their available time on academic work in order to achieve. This not a good predictor for degree level work when the depth and pressure of work increases. Such people could sink under the load. They could be poor planners. If they spend all their time working and their parents provide all the meals and do all the chores they could come very unstuck when living in halls of residence – or worse self-catering accommodation – and have to find time for cooking, personal laundry and possibly cleaning too (cue hollow laughter – students are not known for living in pristine, ideal home type property). They could be poor communicators and have little experience of working with or co-operating with others.

This is why students completing their UCAS and other applications are usually advised by their school or college staff to write something about their extra-curricular interests. Tutors in HEIs do not normally have the slightest interest in whether you are an ardent campanologist or a county standard athlete. What interests them is the fact that you do something that makes demands on your time and proves that you are able to balance conflicting demands on it. If you have a Saturday job or regular sporting commitment now the signs are that you should be able to handle the workload and need for self discipline at higher level study when there will be nobody there to nag and ask whether you have done your homework or finished your assignment. Many admissions tutors in academic subjects will say though that outside interests are irrelevant and all they want is passion for their subject. As there is no way of knowing in advance who they are it is best to play safe and write at least a little about what you do in your spare time. It is even better if you can draw upon these experiences to say which skills and qualities you have gained from them.

The admissions staff who really do want to know about your out of school or college activities are those selecting students for vocational courses. They will want to see evidence of your personal suitability for their course. So:

- Voluntary work can be used as evidence of interest in certain health or social care professions.
- Work experience in industry can be seen as an indication of interest in appropriate careers.
- Voluntary work can also be used to provide evidence of communication, teamwork or leadership skills.
- Boring old 'this is just a job to provide my spending money job' can be used to show reliability, punctuality at the very least and often to prove

that you can accept responsibility. Many allow you to prove that you have people skills and that you can handle tricky situations and difficult customers.

Writing about something you have done over a period of time is also useful. If you have reached grade 6 in an instrument, worked for the same employer or been in the same sports team, drama group or choir for two or more years this suggests that you are not someone who takes up new interests at the drop of a hat and gives them up just as quickly. Perseverance is something else that impresses and points to a student who will not give up easily or keep asking to change options.

It is advisable to concentrate on a few chosen activities and explain what you like about them and how you have benefited from them rather than to simply list a large number of activities with no explanation.

Key words and phrases

- Academic ability
- Enthusiasm
- Relevant knowledge or experience
- Personal suitability
- Time management.

HOW DO ADMISSIONS STAFF FOR COMPETITIVE COURSES SELECT APPLICANTS?

By using the following criteria:

- Known examination results – i.e. GCSE grades and possibly AS module grades. This is a thorny issue since not all schools and colleges reveal these. However, the person writing students' references should add a sentence explaining their policy.
- Predicted grades. Teaching staff are expected to estimate the grades you will achieve in your final examinations.
- Academic reference. This has to be from someone who knows your work and can comment on your attitude to work and your suitability for higher level study. It does not have to be from someone who teaches you. In the college I worked in each subject teacher wrote a paragraph

which was incorporated into a reference written by students' personal tutors. Schools and colleges have their own policies on who writes the final reference. If you are a mature student you need to try to find someone who can comment on your ability to study but all is not lost if you can't. You could well be invited to an interview where you can put your case as this student certainly did: 'At one point he said that he was a little worried about my academic background (I applied from an Access Course as a mature student). I said that I had knowledge of physics, maths and anatomy from that course and also that I was determined to be a radiographer. I said something like "I am a very determined person. I am going to become a radiographer and if you don't offer me a place I will do it somewhere else."'

- Personal statement. More on this later.
- By interview (as one part only of the process). Chapter 7 looks at interviews in detail.

Different Schools/Faculties/Departments – even within the same HEI – use different criteria. They use a mix of the above methods. Some, for instance, do not interview students. Some do, but only in certain cases. Others use known exam results and predicted grades only and simply make offers to those who seem likely to meet their admissions criteria.

Here are some different views.

DEPARTMENT OF MATHEMATICS, UNIVERSITY OF WARWICK, FROM THE UNIVERSITY WEBSITE

'Your UCAS application goes to the University's Student Admissions Office, where it is first considered. (Applications with unusual combinations of subjects are also sent to the Department of Mathematics for further consideration.) If there are no problems (such as not being predicted A in Mathematics) the Admissions Office then send you a formal offer in a letter from the Head of Admissions and relay this to UCAS.'

STEVE WATTS, ADMISSIONS TUTOR FOR HOMERTON COLLEGE, CAMBRIDGE

Steve Watts oversees the admissions procedure for all subjects taught in the college and also selects students for his own subject, English.

'Unlike many universities we interview all the students we think would be suitable for our courses. The interview is an important part but just that, a part of the procedure. There are six criteria we use when selecting students.

'When we receive application forms we look first at the GCSE grades and the A level predictions. On our supplementary application form we will have asked for the percentage scores in all individual modules. These give us a lot more detail and may throw up some questions. For instance if the module score does not tie in with an A grade prediction does the referee comment on or explain this? With this additional information to hand we look in detail at the academic reference. We usually also have the marked essays that candidates have sent in for certain subjects - of which English is one. (Nearly all the colleges teaching English ask for this.) We ask for an essay that has already been marked by the A level teacher and has his or her comments on it. We look at all this information in the context of the school or college. Some applicants may have only relatively few A*s and As at GCSEs for instance, but gained in a school where the average grades are much lower. This marks them out as achievers. The last strand is the applicant's personal statement on the UCAS application. I do use this as part of the process and what I am really looking for is an indication of the applicant's burning wish to do my subject. I am sure that my colleagues in other subjects feel the same way. We are less interested in the applicants' extra-curricular activities than admissions staff in some other universities might be. Because of our interview policy we can get to know a little more about them at that stage. However, this is a very academic place and the overriding factor is academic ability and enthusiasm.

'University statistics show us that the average score across nine AS modules by accepted applicants is about 89%. Most of our applicants are predicted three or four As at A level. We do not reject many without interview and where we do it is usually because the application is not supported by the school or college, mainly regarding their predictions but sometimes also on the reference.'

OXFORD UNIVERSITY, GENERAL STATEMENT FROM THE UNIVERSITY WEBSITE
'Tutors are looking for excellent academic ability and potential, and also for self-motivation and enthusiasm for the degree subject. They look for evidence that you applicants are thinking independently and willing to engage with new ideas, beyond the scope of the school or college syllabus.'

MICHAEL SNAPE, ADMISSIONS TUTOR FOR HISTORY, UNIVERSITY OF BIRMINGHAM

Dr Snape selects students for single honours History and for combined courses in history with economics, social science and war studies.

'When I receive the forms - we are sent paper copies by the University admissions office - I read them through, looking first at the GCSE and AS grades, then the reference and finally the personal statement.

'I am not looking to exclude applicants but we do want students who are going to achieve our entry grades and who will benefit from the courses. Therefore, I am looking for students who genuinely want to study the subject/s. I would only reject those who are clearly unsuited to the courses or who realistically are not likely to get the grades. If a student's predictions are not far below our requirements I sometimes make an offer as an incentive to spur them on. Making offers is a complicated business. You have to offer more places than you have because every student is allowed to make five choices - and you don't know which ones will accept. But the maths usually works out.

'We don't interview because it would be simply too time-consuming.'

VANDA FENN, FACULTY ACADEMIC ADMISSIONS COORDINATOR, SCHOOL OF HEALTH AND SOCIAL CARE, UNIVERSITY OF THE WEST OF ENGLAND, BRISTOL

'The first thing I do is check the UCAS applications to ensure that candidates have the required GCSE passes - it is a requirement of the Nursing and Midwifery Council that students must have English, Maths and a Science (or accepted alternatives). Next I look for predicted grades in the region of 240-280 UCAS points, to include a science subject at 80 points. We accept Physical Education and social sciences such as Psychology and Sociology in this category as well as the laboratory-based science subjects.

'I then read the personal statement. This is the absolutely vital criterion - even more important than the academic ones. (Occasionally if an applicant has an excellent personal statement but is lacking one of the GCSE qualifications I might ring and encourage them to work for level 2 Literacy or Numeracy). I look for insight into the profession. We don't expect work experience. Applicants under 18 are not permitted to do it, so we don't ask for it from anyone, although older applicants may have done it and write about it. Insight means having made the effort to find out about midwifery and the work of midwives. They could have read books on midwifery and professional journals, visited a midwifery department at a university open Day or arranged to go to a local midwifery unit and talked to the staff there about their work. In other words they must have been proactive.

'Applicants should not be including any statement expressing an interest in work with children. If that is their interest, they should be applying for children's nursing or nursery work.

'Applicants that meet the criteria are then sent a biographical questionnaire, which takes 15-20 minutes to complete. This is the BARS questionnaire - Behaviourally Anchored Rating Scale, which works on the premise that past behaviours are indicators of future behaviour. On return the questionnaires are scored by administrative assistants but I look again at the ones that are just below the acceptance score.

'References are read very briefly at the same time as supporting statement. If the applicant has included an inappropriate reference (such as one from a family member/friend), then an academic reference is requested at the same time as biographical questionnaires are sent. After applicants have been interviewed, if they are to be offered a place, then references are scrutinised.

'Successful applicants are then invited to interview.'

HOW USEFUL IS WORK EXPERIENCE?

It can be very useful indeed. Reading about some students' experiences in Chapter 4 you saw how they were able to use examples of what they had learned from them to add value to their applications. There were also some suggestions as to how to arrange a placement.

But what if you can't?

It isn't always possible and people like doctors, vets and lawyers are often overwhelmed with requests from students. In addition they have the problem of contacting patients or clients to ask if they will agree to have a student present.

If you cannot get any experience in the profession you are hoping to enter there are alternatives. You could, for example, visit law courts and observe different kinds of trials. If you cannot arrange work experience in a hospital or with a GP you could try to observe what goes on at a typical GP practice. Perhaps the practice nurse or the receptionist could allow you to spend time with them.

Work experience is important for anyone hoping to enter one of the health care or caring professions (although what we are talking about here is work shadowing rather than experience). But it does not necessarily have to be in the profession itself If you did voluntary work (or paid work if you can get it) in any of the following places you would be able to show that you could work in caring environments and with different kinds of people:

- Children's nursery
- Home for elderly people
- Centre for people with mental or physical disabilities
- Volunteer agencies such as the drug rehabilitation centres or night shelters for the homeless
- The Red Cross.

HOW CAN YOU DEMONSTRATE THAT YOU HAVE THE RIGHT QUALITIES?

Your Personal Statement

When you come to make your application you will be asked to write something in support of your application. On the UCAS application this is known as the personal statement. On other applications it may be known as 'additional information' or 'supporting statement'.

Definitions of these different methods of application are covered in Chapter 2.

You will have realised by now that the personal statement is very, very important. For many admissions tutors it is an essential consideration. Even those who say that they give it relatively little importance often say that they look at it last, rather than not at all, or that they sometimes take it into account if they cannot make up their minds on a candidate's suitability.

What to include in the statement

If you apply to a department that does not normally conduct interviews this could be your only chance to impress the admissions tutors. If the department does interview your personal statement could be one of the factors that gets you to an interview. So plan it carefully.

Admissions tutors need to see here evidence of why you are interested in the courses that you have applied for and evidence of the attributes described at the beginning of the chapter. Before you write your statement it is a good idea to make a list of all the relevant information you can think of and then ask other people who know you well if they can think of anything to add.

The following points are suggested for inclusion:

- What really interests you about this subject, including particular topics that inspire you to want to study it in more depth. Include details of what you have read about the subject *that is not on your exam syllabus*. This can be difficult if you have applied for different courses. HEIs that you apply to will not know what your other choices are – but they will all see the personal statement. This was a problem faced by one student (see page 87) but he managed to write a convincing reason for his choice of both law and history.
- What you hope to get out of studying the subject. This is particularly important if you have chosen a vocational course.
- Why you have chosen a particular course. If all your choices offer the same plus point – perhaps a sandwich placement or the chance to study in another country for part of the course – then can say so. But if only three of your five do so you can't get away with it.
- What career plans you have (if any) for when you complete your course. If you have none as yet, it doesn't matter. Tutors know that students change their minds as they progress through courses and often have very different ideas at the end of three or four years. However, a sentence along the lines of 'I know that this course will enable me to enter the broad career area of X although I have not yet chosen a specific job' or 'I have not yet chosen a career but I realise that this course, as well as being enjoyable, will equip me with a wide range of skills that can be applied to any job' can't do any harm.

- If you are applying for deferred entry explain what you intend to do in your gap year.
- If you are applying for any sponsorships give details of those too.

 TIPS FROM UCAS

On the UCAS website you will find some suggestions for particular qualifications or experiences that you could include:
- Involvement in master classes or other Gifted and Talented programmes
- Details of any accreditation received for your activity in preparation for higher education, for example through the ASDAN Aimhigher Certificate of Personal Effectiveness
- Details of non-accredited skills and achievement that you have gained through activities such as Duke of Edinburgh's Award Scheme, Millennium Volunteers Scheme and Young Enterprise
- Any subjects you are studying that do not have a formal assessment
- Your social, sports or leisure interests
- Your future plans.

In Chapter 4 you were able to see how some students explained their interest in a subject and also drew on various activities and experiences to boost their applications. They used positive sentences that stressed the enthusiasm and commitment tutors are looking for. Here are some examples of good sentences.

Some good sentences to use

Subject related

'Professor P.H Kenny's *Studying Law* has highlighted that not all aspects of law are as glamorous as criminal law and some can be very challenging such as the law of evidence but all are equally important.'

'Visiting my local County Court allowed me to observe the legal system in practice including problems that occur, such as the defendant's failure to attend and how the process of justice is dispensed.'

'I am very keen on applying for Architecture, as I feel that my A level courses give me the perfect grounding for study in this field and I am interested and stimulated by the architectural ideas and work that I have read about, discussed and seen. My Maths and Physics A level courses have given me an excellent basis for the technical parts of an architecture course. Part of my art course was a project featuring styles of buildings, including the Sacre Coeur church, other decorative features from churches and the major new shopping precinct in my local city centre.'

'To broaden my understanding of other historical areas I have joined my school's History Club and the city's Historical Association where I have particularly enjoyed talks on the Holocaust and the Polar Explorations of Captain Scott.'

General skills

'I have completed the Duke of Edinburgh Silver Award. This allowed me to develop my leadership and team building skills. Sport has always interested me as a way of relaxing from academic study. I have represented various teams in netball, hockey and tennis.'

'I have worked part time for three large retailers and at the local leisure centre, and developed my customer service skills.'

'I have further contributed to school life by being an active member of the School Council and Sixth Form Committee, which involves attending regular meetings and communicating with my peers.'

Advice from admissions tutors

**DR IAN GAMESON, SCHOOL OF CHEMISTRY, UNIVERSITY OF BIRMINGHAM,
FROM THE UNIVERSITY WEBSITE**

'You need to show why you want to study a subject. Say "These are the subjects I'm studying at A level and these are the reasons I picked them". Outside interests are also clearly important but don't make them up because these hobbies and interests are a great ice-breaker for an admissions tutor to initiate a conversation.'

LINDA WILSON, ADMISSIONS TUTOR FOR BIOMEDICAL SCIENCES, UNIVERSITY OF LEEDS

'Before applying make sure that you know what you will be studying. This sounds obvious but you may be surprised to know that some students who apply for Pharmacology think this degree will enable them to dispense medicines in a pharmacy. A degree in Pharmacology allows graduates to pursue an exciting career in the pharmaceutical industry researching and developing drug treatment for different medical conditions but you would not be a pharmacist able to dispense drugs. If you want a career dispensing drugs the degree you should be considering is Pharmacy.

'So when you write your personal statement make it obvious that you are aware of what the programme entails. When reading the personal statement of a student applying for Pharmacology I am looking for evidence that the applicant knows what they are applying for. You should justify your choice with an explanation of why the pharmacology degree interests you and give some indication about where you think this may lead in terms of a career.

'Like all the degrees in biomedical sciences, Pharmacology is a good grounding to apply, on graduation, for a place on a postgraduate medicine programme. If this is what you intend to do include this in your personal statement as this shows me that you have undertaken some preliminary research and have a commitment to pharmacology.'

MICHAEL SNAPE, HISTORY, BIRMINGHAM

'My advice to applicants is to make it genuinely your own statement. It needs to be what it says it is - personal. Plagiarism can be an issue. I don't necessarily mean that students buy the statements on offer on the internet but some have obviously been intensively coached. The same words and phrases often crop up.

'You need to tell us why you want to study the course, expressing yourself freely and with independence of thought. Tell me how and why your interest in History extends beyond the A level syllabus. I am not too impressed by some grand claims that begin with "With my school I went on a History trip to X...." That could be from a student who took very little interest in the content of the visit but lived for the evening social life. Tell me instead whether you are a member of a local historical association and what you enjoy about it. Other activities to describe could be membership of a historical re-enactment society or work experience in the heritage industry. Tell me about a strong interest you have, if appropriate, in a period that is totally different from the one you are studying for exams. Other than this, I am not particularly interested in extra-curricular activities other than the fact that they show some balance of time between academic work and other things.'

More good personal statement sentences – general

'During my gap year, I intend to take an industrial placement to apply the skills I have gained and also build upon the current knowledge I have. I feel that by taking this gap year I will gain relevant background knowledge that will act as an advantage to me while studying my course and develop a sense of maturity and also passion towards my career.' *(Sets up possible interview questions for – which you can prepare answers.)*

'I have completed the Millennium Volunteer Scheme which included being a Young Leader at Brownies and I have gained a Duke of Edinburgh's Award which strengthened my team-work and problem solving skills.'

More good personal statement sentences – subject-related

'I enjoyed my work experience at an architect's firm. This placement was organised by my school. I have arranged some further work experience with a different firm for the Christmas holidays, and I will be discussing the construction process with a site manager.'

'I have an interest in many types of art and have visited galleries and exhibitions in London, Paris and New York. I particularly enjoyed writing my personal study of Andy Warhol.'

'To explore what a Psychology degree might entail I read Steven Pinker's *How the Mind Works* which I found fascinating as he takes you on a journey to answer questions such as "Does the parent-offspring conflict begin in the womb?" and "Why did the mass murder in Dunblane happen?"'

Structuring the statement
There are several different layouts you could use.

One is a three paragraph format with one saying why you want to study the subject, a second saying what you enjoy about your present course and the third one about yourself.

Another is to have a new paragraph for each point you mention, i.e. different ones for:

- Subject interest
- Reasons for course choice
- Efforts to find out more about it
- Career plans
- Relevant activities and interests
- Other activities and interests.

BUT there is no set in stone approach. It is your statement and it should be as you want to write it. Schools and colleges usually give advice on structure but don't impose any one model. Some provide examples for different subjects. Others keep copies of former students' personal statements for current students to look at. There are obvious dangers here if you follow the format too closely.

FROM THE UNIVERSITY OF WARWICK'S WEBSITE

'Although we are keen to hear about your work experience and extra- curricular activities, we recommend that you spend no more than a paragraph on them. You also need to think about the structure of your statement. A well-structured, thoughtfully written statement can convey your suitability and commitment to the course by using appropriate information and examples. Finally, make sure your statement reflects you and that you sound interested and interesting!'

FROM THE UNIVERSITY OF BIRMINGHAM'S WEBSITE

'The statement needs to be written by you. The thing to do is to try and really be yourself. It most probably needs a week or so of thought.'

Your last task when composing your personal statement will be to make it the right length. The space allowed for it on the UCAS application is limited. You may need to do several versions, cutting each time until you reach the desired length.

TIP

Your personal statement may be so much part of you by now that you really cannot see any way of changing it. A fresh eye can often spot a sentence that can be shortened or a more concise way of explaining something. Don't be afraid to ask someone or several someones to have a go at editing it for you.

How some students structured their statements (they all received offers)

AMIR HAS APPLIED TO STUDY MATHS AT CAMBRIDGE

'When I wrote my personal statement I wanted to convince the admissions tutors how much I love maths. For me it is a real passion. My first paragraph was about how important I believe that maths is in the world and that all the sciences are defined by it. In my next paragraph I wrote about my achievements in maths. For instance I got a Gold in the UK Maths Challenge and got through the first round in the British Maths Olympiad. I then went on to write about other achievements and interests. For example, I play rugby at county level and both football and tennis for the college.

'I then returned to the subject of maths and described some books I have read about the subject. One in particular is about pi and how some mathematicians have spent over 20 years studying this. I explained that I could fully understand how they could do this because of my own passion and enthusiasm.

'I could have explained that my GCSE grades were not all very high, by the fact that I only came to England from Iran five years ago and started to learn English then. However I knew that this was going to be explained in my college reference so decided not to repeat it. I didn't want to make it look as though I wanted people to feel sorry for me and make me a special case.

'One my separate Cambridge application form I was able to write a lot more specifically about why I wanted to study there.'

LUCIE HAS APPLIED TO STUDY PSYCHOLOGY, WHICH SHE HAS NOT DONE FOR A LEVEL
She felt it was important therefore to impress on admissions tutors how much she had found out about the subject and how it would fit in with her career plans. Her opening sentence was designed to attract immediate attention.

'Will you marry me?' Jo asked a complete stranger. The businessman, who seemed disgruntled by the little girl's interruption, noted her wide-smiling face and as the realisation struck, his features screwed up with disgust. Jo is a teenage girl coping with Downs' Syndrome and for the last 12 months I have been helping her integrate into the community through the Me2Club.'

Lucie then continued in her first paragraph to describe the range of different responses Jo received and how this fuelled her desire to understand the human mind and behaviour through studying Psychology. She went on to write about further experience of working with people who have disabilities.

In her second section she wrote about the steps she had taken to find out what the study of Psychology entailed, naming specific books and what she had found interesting in them. She stressed that she was applying for courses accredited by the British Psychological Society and said that her career aim was to become an educational psychologist.

In a third paragraph she wrote about the aspects of each of her A level subjects that would help her in studying Psychology, and again, named specific examples.

Next came responsibilities, activities and interests. She named positions of responsibility in school, sport, voluntary work and a part-time job as a waitress, drawing out the skills she had gained from each one – communication, initiative, presentations skills, team work, flexibility, patience and resourcefulness. She also used this paragraph to prove that she is good at managing her time as she juggles all these commitments with academic work (and a prediction of high A level grades).

The statement ended with an account of her gap year plans and a final sentence reaffirming her motivation to do a Psychology degree.

Lucie says of the process 'I spent a lot of time on my personal statement - and quite a lot on cutting it down to size. I had a lot to include and it took several attempts to get the wording right. My school keeps a folder containing copies of previous students' personal statements.'

MATTHEW, CURRENT PHYSICS STUDENT AT OXFORD

'I put a fair bit of effort into my personal statement and had a bit of help from my mother and a teacher at my sixth-form college. They didn't write it for me but they made some suggestions and checked the final version before I submitted the application.

'I concentrated largely on my interest in Physics and why I wanted to study it as I thought that was the sort of information admissions tutors would want to see. I wrote about particular areas of A level work that interested me and I went beyond that by writing about some books on Physics that I had read. These were on aspects not covered on the A level course. I also described some work experience I had done at a local science centre and planetarium where children can take part in hands-on interactive science and technology activities. I described what I had done there - a combination of checking equipment in the mornings, helping with the school groups and doing some administrative work. I also wrote about how I felt it was important to give children enthusiasm for science.

'I wrote about some out of college activities. I am not in any college teams but I enjoy playing football and golf. I am also a member of my Area Youth Council which exists to get young people's voices heard locally and also receives a grant to spend on activities. I described my role in that.'

ADAM HAS APPLIED FOR A MIXTURE OF LAW AND HISTORY DEGREES. HE HAS NOW DECIDED ON LAW AND ACCEPTED TWO OFFERS.

Adam put a lot of work into his personal statement. He found it very hard to condense all that he wanted to say but finally managed to get it down to 631 words. Did he have any help from college staff? Yes. 'They did not suggest that I added anything but they were helpful in advising me on some of the wording.'

He had the additional problem of writing a convincing personal statement when applying for two different subjects. How did he do this?

'I started by writing about how the two subjects integrate. I then wrote about Law and History separately. I also include some extra-curricular activities and finally I rounded it off by linking History with Law again. My final sentence was "A career in law is my ultimate goal; both subjects would provide a firm basis for my career aspirations."

Adam organised his statement like this:

1st paragraph
Linking material.

2nd paragraph
Personal opinion on the impact of certain historical events on English law.

3rd paragraph
Interest in law, including evidence from own views on articles written by legal experts in the national press.

4th paragraph
Interest in history, with examples of specific topics.

5th paragraph
Details of a history essay which won the college's Essay Competition; membership of the college History Club with information on talks particularly enjoyed; information on History Master Classes attended at a nearby university and on a visit to Wittenberg where he became more aware of the global influence of Martin Luther.

Adam took great care here to emphasise that he had interests in periods of history not covered in the A level syllabus.

6th paragraph
Activities and responsibilities:

Health Promotion Officer on the Student Association Executive Committee. Completion of the Duke of Edinburgh Bronze Award. Development of leadership and team-building skills.

Sport (as a means of relaxing from academic study and participation in rugby, hockey and tennis teams).

7th paragraph

Skills in analytical techniques and debating acquired from all three A level subjects.

Final paragraph

Final linking statement.

Before adding it to his application Adam justified the entire statement.

One final point

Such is the importance attached to personal statements that there is a brisk trade in plagiarism! Copies of 'good' statements can be bought – and some applicants are apparently so lacking in intelligence that they have copied them word for word.

As a result, UCAS has developed a system known as *Copycatch* which checks all personal statements received against a collection of personal statements already in the Copycatch system and sample statements that have appeared in newspaper articles and on websites. The system looks for a certain level of similarity.

When culprits are found the HEIs they have applied to are notified.

CHAPTER SIX

ADMISSIONS TESTS

Why on earth, you may ask, should you have to take special tests? After all you spend a lot of time working for GCSEs, AS levels and A2s or equivalent qualifications. The answer is that popular universities are deluged with applications from equally well-qualified applicants for their most popular courses. Many students now get straight A grades and the admissions tutors have no way of distinguishing between them. So tests have been devised that reach the parts A levels and Diplomas do not reach.

In some subjects the tests are designed to test other aspects such as personal suitability for the medical profession.

The two most common admissions tests are for law and medicine – at most universities.

MEDICINE

First of all, a definition. Students are often confused by the term 'medical school'. While wearing my careers adviser's hat I have often been asked, 'Is it better to go to a university to study medicine or to a medical school?' The answer is that it is merely a question of terminology. All degree courses in Medicine are held in universities. Some universities call them Faculties of Medicine – as for example 'The Faculty of Medicine, University of Bristol', 'The Faculty of Medicine, University of Sheffield. Others – the majority – call them Schools, as in 'The School of Medicine, Keele University', 'The 'Medical School, Edinburgh' (part of Edinburgh University), 'Hull York Medical School', run jointly by the two universities, 'Peninsula Medical School' at the Universities of Exeter and Plymouth.

If you decide to apply for a place at a medical school you will probably have to take an aptitude test which is designed to test the skills that would-be doctors should possess. You should be aware that if you apply to certain combinations of universities you will have to take two (only three medical schools do not use them at all).

The BioMedical Admissions Test, BMAT

The following universities use BMAT, for **medicine** and for **veterinary science**:

- Cambridge (also for pharmacology)
- Imperial College, London
- Oxford (also for physiological sience)
- The Royal Veterinary College, London
- University College, London.

BMAT is a two hour pencil and paper test consisting of the following papers:

- Aptitude and Skills – short answers or multiple choice, lasts 60 minutes. This is designed to test problem-solving, understanding argument, data analysis and inference
- Scientific Knowledge and Applications – also short answers or multiple choice, lasts 30 minutes. This is based on a knowledge of Double Science and Higher Maths at Key Stage 4
- Writing Task – a short essay from a choice of three titles, lasts 30 minutes. No prior knowledge is required here. You will be expected to develop ideas and explain them effectively.

You must apply to sit the test by the end of September, or up to approximately three weeks later on payment of a penalty fee and you must sit the test on the one date that is offered in any one year. The 2008 date is 5th November. In 2007 it was 31st October and results were given out on 30th November. You may sit the test at your school or college if it is a registered **Assessment Centre** or at an 'Open Centre' (often an independent school that accepts external candidates.) There are test centres in many countries.

The UK Clinical Aptitude Test (UKCAT)

sed by more HEIs than is BMAT – a total of 26 medical and dental schools, namely:

- Aberdeen
- Brighton and Sussex

- Cardiff
- Dundee
- Durham
- East Anglia
- Edinburgh
- Glasgow
- Hull York
- Keele
- King's College, London
- Imperial College, London (for graduate entry)
- Leeds
- Leicester
- Manchester
- Newcastle
- Nottingham
- Oxford (for graduate entry)
- Peninsula Medical School
- Queen Mary, London
- Queen's University, Belfast
- St Andrews
- St George's, London
- Sheffield
- Southampton
- Warwick University (for graduate entry).

UKCAT is a two hour online test consisting of the following sections:

- Verbal Reasoning – this test assesses the ability to think logically about written information and to arrive at a reasoned conclusion. It lasts approximately 20 minutes.
- Quantitative Reasoning – assesses the ability to solve numerical problems. Lasts approximately 20 minutes.
- Abstract Reasoning – this assesses the ability to infer relationships from information by convergent and divergent thinking. Lasts approximately 20 minutes.
- Decision Analysis – you will be expected to deal with different types of information, to infer relationships, to make informed judgements,

and to decide on appropriate responses in complex situations. Lasts approximately 20 minutes.

■ Non-Cognitive Analysis – this looks for 'attributes and characteristics of robustness, empathy and integrity.' Lasts approximately 30 minutes.

All answers are multiple choice.

There is no set date for sitting the test but you must do so by a date in October (10th October in 2007). This is just before the deadline for UCAS applications to medicine. You may register from 1st May to 26th September and take the test from mid-June. Unlike the BMAT test you do not take it at your own school. Instead you have to go to a Pearson Professional Centre (Pearson VUE is the computer-based testing business of Pearson plc which has the contract to administer the UKCAT). There are 150 of these in the UK and others all around the world. You can use the test locator on the UKCAT website, www.ukcat .ac.uk, to find the nearest centre to your home. You should be able to find one no further than 20 miles away – although if you book less than six weeks before you want to take the test you may have to travel 40 miles.

Also on the website you can take a virtual tour of a test centre and see what to expect. If you have already taken your driving test you will already be familiar with the set up since the Pearson company also administers the written part of that test. Basically, you are assigned your own computer terminal and are supplied with a portable whiteboard and pen for making notes.

ANNA WAS ONE OF THE FIRST APPLICANTS TO BE REQUIRED TO TAKE THE UKCAT TEST AND DID SO IN SEPTEMBER

'I was quite nervous about it. It had only just been introduced so I couldn't ask any previous candidates what it was like. I did use the practice questions on the UKCAT website though. They were helpful - particularly in making you realise that you could only use the information given to work out an answer as opposed to giving what you thought was the correct one - but you could spend more time on them than in the actual test. As a result I felt under constant pressure during the real thing and I had to do the last 20 questions very quickly.

'I took the test at a small centre where people also take the written part of the driving test. I was shown into a waiting room where the invigilator gave us each a locker for all our personal belongings. You are not allowed to take anything in with you. He then explained what would happen and we could see through a glass wall into the room where some people were already doing the test, working at individual computer stations and wearing headphones. The stations were rather like the study bays you sometimes see in libraries. We each had a small whiteboard in case we wanted to work any-thing out and each computer had its own calculator. Each section of the test had a briefing page which you could read at your own pace but as soon as you keyed "Next" the timer started and you had to go straight into the questions. As I said, I had to work very fast and I had only just reached the last question when a message saying that time was up appeared on the screen.'

Anna received her results by email approximately four weeks after taking the test. 'We were told that the average score out of a possible 900 marks was 600.' She had scored 580 on Verbal Reasoning, 670 on Quantitative Reasoning, 500 on Abstract Reasoning and 870 on Decision Analysis. Non-Cognitive Analysis has since been added.

LAW

The National Admissions Test for Law
The admissions test for this subject is LNAT or the National Admissions Test for Law.

You will need to take this test if you apply to any of the following universities:

- Birmingham
- Bristol
- Cambridge
- Durham
- Exeter
- Glasgow
- King's College, London
- Nottingham
- Oxford
- University College, London.

LNAT is a two part online test that takes two hours. The first part consists of 30 questions on ten passages with a choice of three multiple choice answers for each question. This part takes 80 minutes and is designed to test powers of:

- Comprehension
- Analysis
- Interpretation
- Synthesis
- Induction
- Deduction – in other words you will be providing evidence of the verbal reasoning skills required to study and practise law.

The essay part takes 40 minutes and will require you to write around 500 to 600 words (guidelines say no more than 750) on a topic from a choice of several. You do not require any particular knowledge other than 'a rudimentary knowledge of everyday subjects' but will be expected to argue to a conclusion in good written English.

There is much more information on the LNAT website, www.lnat.ac.uk, where you can find out more about the different parts of the test and read some tips on both tackling multiple choice questions and writing the kind of essay that will impress. For instance you are told that LNAT assessors are not interested in your opinions but in your ability to defend an argument.

The test is written by Edexcel.

There is no set date for sitting the test but you may take it from 1st September and may register to do so from 1st August. LNAT strongly recommends that you sit the test by 20th January if you submit your UCAS application by 15th January and by 1st November if you apply to Oxford or Cambridge. These dates fit with the deadlines for UCAS applications.

The LNAT is administered, by Pearson VUE at one of their test centres. If your interest is in law you are likely to have skipped the bit about Pearson testing in the paragraphs on UKCAT, so although this is repetition, here is how it works. You do not take the test at your own school. Instead you have to go to a Pearson Professional Centre (Pearson Vue is the computer-based testing business of Pearson plc which has the contract to administer the LNAT). There are 150 of these in the UK and others all around the world. You can use the test locator on the LNAT website, to find the nearest centre to your home. You should be able to find one no further than 20 miles away although if you book less than six weeks before you want to take the test you may have to travel 40 miles.

Also on the website you can take a virtual tour of a test centre and see what to expect. If you have already taken your driving test you will already be familiar with the set up since the Pearson company also administers the written part of the test. Basically, you are assigned your own computer terminal and are supplied with a portable whiteboard and pen for making notes.

CAN YOU PREPARE FOR BMAT, UKCAT AND LNAT?

You cannot learn or revise anything for these tests. However, you can certainly prepare for them by finding out what to expect and familiarising yourself with equipment in the case of computer-based tests.

Needless to say the minute that a new aspect of the higher education application process is devised, along come a host of organisations offering to coach students for it (at a price). You can find details of these online (I found several within seconds after keying 'BMAT Preparation' into Google). Prices ranged from £70–£260.

Cambridge Assessment, the organisation that sets BMAT says that critical thinking can be taught, and that practice will improve this skill. It does not regard training courses as necessary. In fact it is quite scathing about them, saying 'Please note – companies offering help with BMAT do not have a special insight into the nature of the test and indeed the logic of some of the claims published on their websites is basically faulty. While a candidate's performance at any test will improve with some familiarisation or practice, anyone looking to pay for such practice should consider very carefully about whether they are wasting their money. It does recommend its own book, *Preparing for the BMAT: The Official Guide to the BioMedical Admissions Test* which contains specimen questions, written by the people who set the tests plus recommended approaches and worked examples. You could buy this from a former student perhaps, or from an internet bookstore.

You can also practise test questions on the BMAT website, www.bmat.org.uk. This site also contains detailed information on the test and recommended books to help you to develop further some of the necessary skills.

UKCAT is equally dismissive of training courses, saying 'The university Medical and Dental Schools participating in UKCAT do not endorse any commercially available preparation course for the UKCAT. Preparation is not necessary, desirable or advantageous.'

However, you are advised to practise answering the types of questions that you will be asked in the UKCAT, and to get used to the question styles, multiple-choice format and requirements of each subtest. You can do all this free of charge on the UKCAT website as well as getting used to moving the mouse and moving through the test. On the website you will find both an online demonstration and practice questions to download.

LNAT too dismisses training courses, stating 'We advise you to be sceptical about anyone's claims to be able to help you do well in the test by coaching. Instead, do your own preparation free.' and 'The advice you will be given if you pay someone for LNAT preparation is mostly common sense. Why pay? Here is the same advice for free.' Multiple choice and essay hints follow. You can do a timed practice test on the LNAT website.

Nevertheless, you may feel that attendance at a day's training course could be helpful – especially if you know other people who are going to do this and don't want to feel that you are missing out on what they are getting. If you look at the prices and feel that they are beyond your means you could follow the advice of one of the test organisers which says 'If you are a student who can't afford to come on one of our Training Days we offer this advice:

- Ask your teacher about the Gifted and Talented funds available at your place of education. Schools have money especially set aside for you. If you are applying for medicine you count as Gifted or Talented!
- Use your EMA (Education Maintenance Allowance).
- Contact us in the strictest confidence: we do have allocated means to help you.'

OXFORD AND CAMBRIDGE

As you are doubtless aware, these two universities are so popular that they are always oversubscribed. Add to that the fact that schools usually suggest that only students who are certain to get A grades should apply and you can see immediately that they have tremendous selection problems. In fact, Dr Mike Sewell, Admissions Tutor at Selwyn college, Cambridge, was quoted in *The Independent* in November 2007 as saying that the painful part of his job was having to disappoint 'three out of four very talented and usually very nice 17 year olds, most of whom have never failed at anything before.' So – for a long time these two universities have had their own admissions tests, ones containing questions that are intended to go deeper than A level ones. They also conduct interviews (more on these in Chapter 7). Even so, Cambridge has to turn away 5,000 students with straight As at A level every year. The clear message is that if you decide to try for 'Oxbridge' and are not accepted you are far from being a failure!

The tests

Cambridge STEP

What is STEP (Sixth Term Examination Papers in Mathematics)? It is an additional exam that is taken in the sixth term of Year 13.

STEP consists of three papers that are used to supplement GCE A levels. If you are taking single Maths A level you will normally be asked to take STEP papers 1 and 2. If you are taking Maths and Further Maths you will normally be asked to take papers 2 and 3. You apply to take STEP through your school or college.

Questions are based on material that is already included in A level Mathematics, so do not require any further knowledge, and are, says the university 'of a searching kind designed to test qualities like insight, originality, grasp of broader issues and the ability to use standard techniques in unusual ways and situations.' Individual colleges see the papers and can assess particular strengths or weaknesses as opposed to simply having the overall mark.

You will receive a mark as follows:

- S (Outstanding)
- 1, 2 and 3 (Satisfactory).

Colleges decide which grades to ask for when making a conditional offer. They use STEP as part of conditional offers for maths and sometimes for other subjects. For example, Churchill College may use it for engineering and computer science, Magdalene for computer science and Peterhouse for engineering.

You can get past papers from OCR Publications, which can also supply you with a *STEP Regulations and Specifications* booklet. If you are at a school or college your maths teachers will have this already. You will also find some information on the Faculty of Mathematics website, www.maths.cam.ac.uk/undergrad/admissionsinfo.

Other admissions tests are used by individual colleges for certain subjects. This is a college as opposed to university-wide decision. Therefore some colleges may set a test at interview as part of their selection process while another college selecting applicants for the same subject may rely on interviews alone. Common tests or additional selection methods include those detailed below.

Thinking Skills Assessment

You may be asked to do the Thinking Skills Assessment Test either online or on paper when you go to Cambridge for an interview. It is designed to assess critical thinking and problem-solving skills, and as it is not specific to particular subjects it can be applied to several courses. Some Cambridge colleges use it to assess applicants for computer science, economics, engineering, land economy and natural sciences.

More information and examples of TSA questions can be found on the TSA website at: www.tsa.cambridgeassessment.org.uk.

Essays

Students who apply for arts and social science courses are often asked to send essays that they have already written as part of their A level course.

They have to be original and already marked by teachers, showing the marking and comments. Individual colleges will tell you if they wish you to send such work to them.

Cambridge University also requires applicants to sit BMAT or LNAT as appropriate.

Oxford

Many Oxford colleges also expect applicants to sit additional exams. This depends on the college and the subject. There is no one entrance exam for Oxford as a university. Currently you will have to do so if you are applying for any of the following subjects:

- Computer Science
- English (ELAT, English Literature Admissions Test)
- History (HAT, History Aptitude Test)
- Law (LNAT)
- Mathematics
- Medicine (BMAT)
- Physics – applicants must take a two hour long test in physics and an additional two hour one in mathematics for physicists
- Physiological Sciences
- PPE (Politics, Philosophy and Economics). Oxford uses the Thinking Skills Aptitude Test for this subject.

Many of these tests are described in detail on the Oxford website.

All the tests except BMAT and LNAT are taken at the end of October. If you are at a school or college you will sit them there and need not register separately as teaching staff will do this for you. If you are an external applicant you need to take the tests at a registered centre – you can find out where these are from the university.

Some subjects also have additional tests which are taken at Oxford when you go for interview. For instance you would:

- Do written translations for classical and modern languages courses.
- Do a drawing examination for fine art.

- Take a language aptitude test for beginners' Russian.
- Take a test designed to demonstrate ability to reason analytically for philosophy.

You can find out which subjects do have tests in the university prospectus or on the course pages on the Oxford website, www.admissions.ox.ac.uk where you will also find specimen tests.

Written work

Admissions tutors in most subjects expect to see samples of written work – which must be sent to colleges by 10th November. Typically you will be asked to send one or two marked coursework essays.

Most subjects have a written work or test requirement, some have both. The list is too long to give here but can be found on the website, www.admissions.ox.ac.uk. The only subjects which do not have either a written test at interview or a requirement to send in samples of written work are:

- Biochemistry
- Biomolecular Science
- Chemistry
- Earth Sciences
- Engineering, Economics and Management
- Engineering Science
- Material Science
- Materials, Economics and Management.

Other HEIs

Some other universities and colleges also expect to see samples of written work from applicants to certain courses. Sometimes students are expected to send them. Sometimes they are asked to take them to an interview.

For example:

- Many HEIs offering journalism degrees expect to see a portfolio of articles or set an advance assignment.
- Some send out questionnaires to psychology applicants.

■ The LSE asks applicants for social policy to send two essays.

■ The Royal Welsh College of Music says, 'Please bring photocopied examples of recent written work such as essays, analyses or harmony exercises, which you can leave with us to look at after your audition. You might also wish to bring any examples of your own compositions. Please do not bring large portfolios.' (For applicants for composition)

USEFUL SOURCES OF INFORMATION

Websites

www.admissions.ox.ac.uk

www.bmat.org.uk

www.cam.ac.uk/admissions/undergraduate

www.lnat.ac.uk

www.ukcat.ac.uk

www.tsa.cambridgeassessment.org.uk.

Addresses

OCR Publications, PO Box 5050, Annersley, Nottingham NG15 0DL.

Email: publications@ocr.org.uk

CHAPTER SEVEN
INTERVIEWS AND AUDITIONS

It is by no means the case that you will be called for an interview at your chosen HEIs. Many simply don't use them as part of their selection process. There is not usually an HEI-wide policy – staff in individual departments normally make the decision. So you could find that you had not been invited to an interview at a certain HEI whereas one of your friends had. This is neither a good sign nor a bad one, or any reflection on either of you. It is simply a matter of policy.

❝Once we have considered your application we may invite you to come for an interview, but like many other universities and colleges we do also make decisions without interview. (If you receive an offer without interview we will invite you to an Open Day at which you will be able to make a more informed judgement about what we have to offer you.)❞
UNIVERSITY OF DURHAM

❝Applicants are often surprised when they receive an offer before they visit us. We make a virtue of giving a standard offer because:

- It is a completely transparent policy and
- We know that those who achieve it ALL have the potential to get the best from our degree courses.❞

DEPARTMENT OF MATHEMATICS, UNIVERSITY OF WARWICK

Sometimes it is simply a matter of time, for example:

❝We don't interview because it would be simply too time consuming. I and my colleagues would be tied up doing nothing else for several weeks. (This year we received 900 applications for 150 places on the four programmes.)**❞**
DR MICHAEL SNAPE, DEPARTMENT OF HISTORY, UNIVERSITY OF BIRMINGHAM

❝ We do not normally interview non-mature candidates, although this may happen in exceptional cases.**❞**
FROM BRISTOL UNIVERSITY SCHOOL OF LAW'S WEBSITE

What are exceptional cases?

This definition often includes:

- Mature candidates
- Applicants with an unusual educational background
- 'Borderline cases' – whose predicted grades may not be as high as the entry requirements dictate but who have very supportive references.

Other than those in the above categories you are likely to be interviewed if:

- You are applying for a new subject
- You are applying for a course that is directly linked to a particular career, and in many cases forms the first part of the necessary training for it
- You are applying to Oxford or Cambridge.

WHAT HAPPENS IN AN INTERVIEW?

This varies from HEI to HEI, or rather with individual Schools/Faculties/ Departments. Some are conducted by just one person; others by two; and some even by a small panel. As you will see when you read on, personal interviews may take up only a small part of a selection process that also includes practical assessments, group exercises, discussions and debates. Often this type of process is combined with a departmental Open Day, presentations on the course, visits and the chance to talk to current students.

Some interviews are very informal. Several students interviewed for this book described them as 'more like a friendly chat'. Others contain technical questions, possibly on some aspects of your exam syllabus; more often they can be questions that are designed to go beyond what you have studied already and are designed to make you think a problem through. Usually, as well as being interested in your res ponses the interviewer is looking at the ways in which you think and the reasoning that you do in order to reach an answer. Often there are no right or wrong answers.

There is no standard interview format. However, an interviewer may begin by asking you about some of the things you wrote on your personal statement. This is within your comfort zone. You know what you wrote and can expand on this to provide further information. He or she may begin by asking about your journey or by talking about the activities and interests you put on the personal statement. This to put you at ease and allow to relax a little.

Very often the interview is based on the personal statement and follows it closely. Several students referred to this. *It is absolutely vital to remember what you wrote!*

Some typical interview questions

- Why do you want to come here?
- Why should we give you a place?
- Are you a leader?
- Can you work in a team?
- Give me an example of something that you have achieved in the past year.
- Have you been to one of our Open Days?
- What have you read outside the A level syllabus?
- Why did you have a poor grade in GCSE Maths/French/Geography?
- What do you do in your spare time?

- What skills have you learned from your part-time employment?
- Tell us some more about your work experience at X.
- Tell me more about the drama group/hockey team/Saturday job you wrote about on your application?
- Have you any questions for us?

Interviews always include the opportunity for you to ask questions. It is a good idea to have some ready. There is nothing wrong with writing them down and taking the list with you. Asking questions shows interest, but if you have none, say so. *Whatever you do, do not ask anything that you could have found out from the website or in the course descriptions.* To prove that you have done thorough research about the course you can always say something like 'No thank you your website was very detailed and gave me all the information I need', (flattering) or 'I spoke to someone about the course at your Open Day and had all my questions answered then' (proves you have been thinking about this course for some time). If your questions are answered either during a presentation or even during the interview itself you could say, 'Thank you. I did have questions about X, Y and Z but they have been answered today'.

Some more typical questions

Course or subject-related

- Why do you want to do this subject/be a barrister/be a doctor?
- What qualities do you think a successful doctor/engineer/ surveyor should have?
- Do you possess them?
- Have you read about any legal cases in the last few weeks?
- What is the role of the architect in society?
- What changes in the landscape did you notice on your journey here? (geography, environmental studies)
- What transport problems are there in your home area? (planning, geography)
- What stereotypes do we have about people with mental illness here? (psychology)
- What is a philosophical question?

- Have any important advances been made in the biological field recently?
- Should nurses go on strike?
- How would you feel if you had to promote a product that you did not personally like? (advertising, marketing)
- What causes a volcano?
- What do you think of the selection of novels made for the last Booker Prize?
- Is the power of the prime minister increasing? (politics)
- Describe a recent practical to me.
- What makes a good manager? (business studies).

What you will not get are any trick questions. Interviewers do not try to catch you out. You may have heard the (ancient) story of the Oxbridge interviewer who said in a bored tone 'Surprise me' and retreated behind a newspaper. The candidate promptly set it alight. Most current interviewers have received training in interview technique. I have myself been told by an admissions tutor for biology that he often throws an egg (hard boiled – but then the candidate does not know that!) to the candidate and says 'Describe this to me' – but then that comes into the category of making you think on the spot, doesn't it?

Interviewers are trying to get to know you as a person. They are trying to assess whether you:

- Will be able to cope academically with the course
- Are sufficiently interested in it (passion, commitment and enthusiasm again)
- Have the right personal qualities – in the case of a vocational courses
- Have the right practical or technical skills
- Will benefit from the course.

However, most say that they are not looking for reasons to reject candidates. They simply want the right students on their courses. It is in nobody's interests, least of all students', to be given places on courses they will not cope with or enjoy. They will only drop out.

Assessment

Quite often, the interviewer has a checklist of points to look for, drawn up by colleagues. These can include:

- Did the candidate maintain eye contact throughout the interview?
- Was s/he enthusiastic and well-motivated?
- Does s/he communicate well?
- Did s/he demonstrate commitment to the subject?
- Has s/he taken steps to find out about X as a career?

A new subject

If you are applying for a subject that you have not done before, admissions tutors need to be sure that you understand what you are letting yourself in for. You could be well be invited to an interview and asked questions designed to find out just how much you know about the subject and what steps you took to find out. So you can expect to be asked first of all how you became interested in the subject and which books you have read about it for instance. This is not always the case though. Many admissions tutors are happy to gain this information from personal statements rather than hold interviews.

ALEX IS STUDYING TRANSPORTATION DESIGN AT NORTHUMBRIA UNIVERSITY

This is not a university that features in any 'top ten' or 'top twenty' lists but this particular course is one that has an excellent success rate for graduate employment. This is a reminder that the best courses are not always in the universities that score highly *overall* in league tables!

'I was interviewed by a lecturer who had worked in the car industry (and is now my personal tutor). He asked me first about my reasons for wanting to do the course and I did my best to explain about how exciting I found design work. I tried hard to avoid phrases like "I have loved cars for ever" and tried to get my passion for design across.

'We also talked about my interest in cars but more specifically in yacht design. It turned out that he loved boats and yachts too so he asked me a lot of questions to test my knowledge. Luckily I was able to name some names, for example Sunseeker Power Yacht, Fairline and Aquariva a small firm that builds some of the most exclusive power boats in the world and explain why I admired their products.

'He looked through my portfolio too of course and asked me a lot of questions about why I had chosen certain topics, why I had done the pieces in a particular way and so on. It was a very relaxed atmosphere though, an enjoyable experience in fact and I felt as though I was chatting to a fellow enthusiast'

PREPARING FOR INTERVIEWS

A good way to prepare for your interview is to read widely around your chosen subject. Be ready to talk about something that is outside and/ or deeper than your A level subjects. Read newspaper articles, websites, professional journals and magazines. Read a quality national newspaper and be informed about current affairs – especially if they are relevant to your subject or course.

- Re-read your personal statement
- Re-read any written work that you had to send in and be prepared to be questioned on it.

Practice interviews

It can be a good idea to find someone who will hold a practice interview with you. If it is for an academic subject the ideal person would be someone who teaches that subject but who does not teach you. That way you will be discussing with a subject expert but will also be getting used to doing so with a stranger.

❛ I prepared answers to lots of possible questions and I had a practice interview with my college's vice principal who said I had done well and gave me some confidence.❜
CURRENT APPLICANT

A course that is directly linked to a particular career

This usually also comes into the new subject category. Included in this section are courses such as architecture, law, medicine, engineering, those leading to qualification in caring or health care professions etc.

Here the interviewer is not only assessing students for the ability to succeed on a particular course but also to work in the relevant profession. They will be looking for specific skills and qualities – and the interview may include some questions related to that career. Often, a person working in that profession may be one of the interviewers. Frequently, a short interview is only a small part of a selection day or half day at which students have to do some practical tests and assessments.

VANDA FENN, FACULTY ACADEMIC ADMISSIONS COORDINATOR, SCHOOL OF HEALTH AND SOCIAL CARE, UNIVERSITY OF THE WEST OF ENGLAND, BRISTOL EXPLAINS THEIR SYSTEM

'Successful applicants (following the initial screening process described in Chapter 5) are invited to interview. Two people, one a member of the School's academic staff and the other a practising midwife, conduct the interviews which are based on past experiences. They will ask questions such as "What have you done as part of a team" or "Can you describe a situation in which you had to deal with someone who was behaving angrily or aggressively towards you?"

'Both interviewers score the candidate's performance and successful applicants are offered places.'

SOME MORE STUDENTS' EXPERIENCES

RISHI HAS APPLIED FOR AERONAUTICAL ENGINEERING

'I had three interviews. Each one was different.

'Bristol was the most technical. They asked the obvious questions like "Why this course?" and "Why this university?" and then moved on to subject-related questions. They asked me several questions - one was on why a wing generates lift, when subject to airflow - and went much more deeply into the physics behind my answers. They also asked about my air cadet experience and about the Engineering Education Scheme project.

'Loughborough and Surrey were much less formal - more like a friendly chat. They explored my motives again and asked a lot about my experiences in both my student and extra-curricular life.'

ANNA, MEDICAL STUDENT, DURHAM UNIVERSITY

'Durham was where I had decided I really wanted to go and I would much rather have had an interview somewhere else first for the practice! The interview wasn't quite what I had expected. It was with the admissions secretary of the medical school and a local doctor. They hadn't seen my UCAS application so they knew nothing about me and asked the sort of questions they felt they needed to in order to establish whether I would make a good doctor. This is the standard practice there and they explained to me that it was in order to stop them feeling any prejudice or bias.' (Anna had however, been selected for interview on the basis of what was written in her UCAS application.)

'They asked me some of the questions I had been expecting like why I wanted to be a doctor, why I had chosen Durham, why I felt they should offer me a place, what qualities I thought a doctor should possess but not much on my A level subjects on science or on current issues – all of which I had been asked in my mock interview. They also asked for an example of my teamwork skills – I used netball for this – and to describe a situation I had found difficult. I didn't want to sound negative so I thought quickly and said that I had found settling in to sixth-form college quite hard but that I had persevered.

'Then there were two scenario questions. I had to read a card which told me that two of my best friends were seeing each other and that one had confided in me that they were cheating on the other person. I had to read this with the interviewers watching me and I found this quite hard. I then had to say what I would do with the information and I said that much as would have liked to warn my friend I had to respect the other friend's confidence. The second scenario was about whether to advise a pregnant patient who had a strong chance of giving birth to a baby with a handicap whether or not to have a test carried out. The procedure would contain a risk of miscarriage. I first said that I would give the patient all the information as clearly and compassionately as I could and leave the decision to her – but they said that I had to offer advice. So I said that I thought that the test should be advised. The doctor then said to me "How would you feel if the baby died?" so I thought I must have given the wrong answer. However, I discovered later he had asked another applicant who had given the opposite answer how she would feel if the baby was born with a severe handicap.

'I came out thinking that I could have done better but that I hadn't made any ghastly errors.'

Anna had one other interview – at East Anglia where the system was different. A small group of applicants are shown into the interview room where they find a series of booths, known as 'stations'. There are seven stations to move through and candidates spend five or six minutes at each station.

'We each selected a station and went to it. When the time was up a whistle blew and we all went back to our seats for a minute or two while the interviewers graded our performance and they wrote the marks on to score sheets. Then we went to all the other stations in turn. This time the assessors had our UCAS applications in front of them. Some of the questions involved scenarios again. One was about how to help a friend who was under pressure and another was about a patient who was not taking prescribed medication. At other stations I was asked why they should select me, why I had chosen to apply there, about my ability to work in a team and about my work experience.'

DIVYA HAS APPLIED FOR CIVIL ENGINEERING

'I had interviews at all my five universities. They differed in structure. The first one was at Warwick. This was a 15 minute one with one person who asked fairly general questions about my reasons for wanting to be a civil engineer and asked me about some of the things I had written in my personal statement.

'Imperial was next. This was by far the most technical one. In the morning the candidates were divided into groups of four and set projects to do. In the afternoon I had a 25 minute interview with a Geotechnics specialist. The interviewer was very nice and started by asking me some general questions like my reasons for choosing the course and the place, then moved on to ask me things related to the morning project. She then asked some technical questions on Physics.

'At UCL we worked in groups where they asked us to solve a given problem. We then presented this to another group working on the same problem. We worked out by ourselves how we would present our problem and solution to the other group, by dividing it into sections. I didn't have a one to one interview.

'At Bath the one to one interview was one part of a departmental Open Day. We had a campus tour, saw the accommodation and had lunch. There was a problem solving exercise here too. This time, working in small groups we had to construct a tower out of drinking straws and Blu-Tack that would support a given weight. My interview was amazing. As soon as I went in the interviewer told me that they were going to offer me a place and then for the remainder of the time we talked about the course. He told me about some aspects of it and let me ask questions. He even ended by advising me how to apply for bursaries.

'Manchester also included tours and a subject talk. I had a one to one interview but there were no problems or tasks set. I was asked a few technical questions - mainly on a school project I had done and on Physics.

JULIE IS STUDYING DIAGNOSTIC RADIOGRAPHY AT CANTERBURY CHRIST CHURCH UNIVERSITY

'At UCL I had a tour, a talk about the course and an individual interview. There was also a task to complete. Working in small groups we had to do a project and were told in advance which sections we would each give a presentation on. That was obviously assessed.

'I was offered interviews at all my choices but in fact only went to two. I was then in a position to make my decisions.

'At Canterbury Christ Church University the selection process, which included an interview, lasted a whole day. When I arrived I and the other applicants were given an introductory talk and a guided tour of the department. Then came a practical test. We were shown into a room where ten X-rays were laid out on tables. We had to examine them all and write descriptions of what we had found out from them. This was a test of both powers of observation and of written communication skill. After lunch we sat and waited to be called for our individual interviews. This was the most nerve-wracking part of the day.

'In my interview, which was with one of the senior lecturers, I was asked about my reasons for wanting to do Radiography. I expanded on some of the things I had written on my personal statement and explained that I had first become interested in the profession when I had had MRI and CT scans following an accident. I had seen the job from the patient's viewpoint then and had arranged to visit a radiography department later to learn more about the work.

'I also said that I thought I had the right skills for the job. I had worked in retail both as a sales assistant and a manager and had also worked as a care officer with people with Downs Syndrome and autism. I talked about how my experience had developed my communication and caring skills.

'The one at City was very different. We had a short introductory talk and then almost immediately the lecturers left and two students - one in Diagnostic Radiography and one in Radiotherapy came in to talk to us. They each described their own specialism - in a very amusing way, each saying how their one was better - and then answered any questions we had.

'We had a tour of the department and were able to handle the X-ray machinery, then had two practical tests before the individual interviews. First we did an observation and communication exercise. We sat back to back in pairs, each facing an overhead projector with a picture on it. I can still see mine. It was a house with a cross in the middle. We each had to describe the picture to our partners - who had to draw it. Then we compared the drawings with the originals.

'The part that I enjoyed most was a short debate. We all had to pick a topic out of a hat and speak on the subject for five minutes. Mine was equality and lasted for ten minutes because once I had started it went very well and I generated a very lively discussion!'

An academic subject

If you want to study an academic subject, whether this is a familiar one such as English, geography, history or maths or a new one like philosophy you might not have an interview. It is quite likely that a decision will be made using your exam predictions, reference and personal statement.

If you are interviewed however, expect most of the questions to be on the subject and be ready to demonstrate the key qualities again. The interviewer could well be teaching you next year and will be looking for the ideal student – someone who is burning to study this particular subject in depth and who will make a positive contribution to class discussion.

SOME INTERVIEW TIPS

Before the interview
Do
- Keep a hard copy of your UCAS application and re-read it just before or on your way to the interview.
- Make notes on anything that has changed. For example – did you mention that you were in the process of arranging some work experience but in fact were unable to do so? Be ready to explain that it didn't come off but that you tried very hard.
- If anything in your exam work has changed be ready to talk about that too. For instance have you decided not to complete that extra AS subject?
- Find out how to get to the HEI from the station or where you can park if going by car.
- Allow plenty of time to get there – more than you think is necessary.
- If something beyond your control delays your journey – late train, motorway hold-up, accident etc – phone and explain.
- Get there early. You can then find the interview room without getting flustered and can sit down and try to relax.
- Do expect to feel nervous. Everyone does and interviewers make allowances for nerves.

At the interview
Do
- Speak clearly.
- Answer the question that is asked, even if you would like to show what you know about the topic. It's the same advice you are given about answering exam questions, isn't It?
- If you don't understand the question don't be afraid to ask the interviewer to repeat or rephrase it.
- If there is more than one person conducting the interview – when you answer look directly at the person who asked you the question but from time to time look at the other person too. This includes them – and they are listening too.

Don't
- Try to answer a question too quickly. Think about it.
- Answer just 'Yes' or 'No'.
- Talk too much. If you give a clear and concise answer the interviewers can decide whether that is sufficient or if they want more. If so they will continue on this topic. Let them steer the conversation.

- Criticise your school or college. If you had three changes of teacher last year this should be mentioned in your reference and they will have noted this. Check with the person who wrote the reference that this has been done! Ideally they should discuss this with you at the time.
- Bluff. If you really don't know the answer to a question it is better to admit it. Otherwise you will get into difficulties if the questions become more detailed.
- Pretend you know about something when you don't. It could be very embarrassing for you if you are questioned on it in depth.

OXFORD OR CAMBRIDGE

These two universities make heavy use of the interview despite their large numbers of applicants. Why?

Because both receive applications from exceptionally able candidates with predicted top grades, usually very supportive references and very good personal statements. Therefore they find it extremely difficult to choose between applicants fairly. Cambridge says 'All of this makes comparing applicants on paper, on a formulaic basis, problematic. Interviews help by allowing us to go beyond the paperwork. However, the most important purpose of interviews is to allow us to judge whether an applicant has chosen the right subject/course, and has the potential to study it to a very high level and whether the Cambridge course is well suited to an applicant's particular interests and aptitudes'. You will find this and more on the Cambridge website. Oxford too has a section on interviews on its website. Both universities offer advice on how to preparefor them.

YOU WILL ALREADY HAVE READ SOME ADVICE FROM STEVE WATTS OF HOMERTON COLLEGE, CAMBRIDGE IN CHAPTER 5. THIS WHAT HE SAYS ABOUT INTERVIEWS

'Students come to Cambridge for one day but those from further afield may stay overnight if they wish. Sometimes they have a gap between practical tests and interviews and it is good for them to have somewhere to go back to as a base if they wish to do so.

'Practical tests or written work are set by most colleges and in most subjects. Applicants for English are sometimes given a written test; sometimes an oral test within the interview when they are asked to read through a passage then answer questions on it. The written test might consist of comparing and contrasting two poems - as could happen in an English class here.

'History staff do a similar exercise using written passages or a collection of historical sources. At Homerton candidates for English are given one hour to read a passage and then write a practical criticism (commentary) on it. The answers are marked immediately by some tutors while others begin the first of the two interviews.

'Most interviews are conducted by two people. We think that is fairer to the students. Interviews for arts subjects are based on discussion. We also discuss the written work, from which we can also assess their ability to write under pressure. We usually ask them for a list of books they have read recently that have made a real impact on them and ask them to explain why. If they say that it was a good book - how do they define 'good'? Was it purely the subject matter that interested them? They will probably be asked questions about texts they have mentioned in their personal statements. I might well ask them about the texts they have not mentioned, but have studied, as well and ask them to explain why. Is it because they do not like them? Why not?

'At least 50% of interview time will be spent in taking students out of their comfort zone and forcing them to think more deeply about issues.

'After the interview the four interviewers have to compare notes and make their lists of students to whom they would like to offer places. Then come admissions meetings. As admissions tutor for the college I attend them all - and I know that as with my subject these discussions can last for hours. Normally there will be agreement over the students we are sure of. It is equally easy to agree on the ones who will not get offers. The middle band is the problem - when you have a limited number of places left and too many students in the category. We do our best to agree and give each one a score. However, we then wait for the Pool list to become available and look through the applications of some well-qualified candidate who have not been made offers by other colleges in case we find some who have higher score than some of our own middle band ones. In a normal year we make offers to a fairly high percentage of Pool candidates.'

Two students

AMIR HAS APPLIED TO STUDY MATHS AT CAMBRIDGE

'I prepared for the interview by thinking of the types of questions I might be asked and I also read the file that my college keeps for us to use. Every student who attends an interview is asked to write about it and put their account in the file.

'I spent one day in Cambridge and had two interviews, each one with one person. The first one was concerned with my knowledge. He gave me a couple of problems to solve and watched me do them. He was looking at my ability to answer questions and my analytical ability. He also went through one question with me getting to the solution in a different way and watched how quickly I could the same.

'The second one was not so mathematically challenging. He said that he was interested in how my mind worked. One question was about integrating sin^5x with respect to x from pi to minus pi. You can use De Moivre's theorem to put sin^5x in term of trigonometry that you can integrate but if you spend one minute thinking about the question you will see that sin^5x is an odd function therefore it has rotational symmetry of order of two around the origin hence integrating from pi to minus pi sin5x with respect to x is 0.

'I was a little bit nervous before the interviews. The worst bit was waiting outside the interview room with all the other candidates. Nobody said very much. When I got inside I found that I was able to relax and concentrate on Maths.'

Other questions Amir was asked at interview:

- Why do you want to study Mathematics and why here?
- Which field of Mathematics are you particularly interested in?

MATTHEW IS STUDYING PHYSICS AT MERTON COLLEGE, OXFORD

'Oxford interviews take place at the end of the autumn term when the students have gone, and you spend one or more nights in college. I was quite nervous but I had had a mock interview at college and I knew what to expect. When I got there I found it to be a very good experience. Everyone was very relaxed and friendly – even the other candidates. Technically of course, we were in competition with each other but we all got on very well.

'I had three separate interviews and in each one I was asked about topics I hadn't done before. I was given questions for instance on aspects of mechanics, energy or friction that were new to me. In all three interviews I could tell that the interviewers were trying to assess how I dealt with a question, how I thought things through to a conclusion and how good my analytical ability was. It wasn't so much that my answer was important – rather how I got to it The interviews were really like mini tutorials. I was led through the exercise by the tutors who questioned me and added points for me to consider. They wanted to see how I responded to them and whether I could take them on board.'

Matthew had one more interview – at Imperial College, London. This was a completely different experience in that it was a group interview with five other students who discussed questions a group.

MORE TIPS

Try not to give vague answers such as 'I like reading' (what do you read and why?) and 'I like socialising' (this is not relevant and also suggests that your priorities may be wrong!).

The following are *not* considered good replies!

- I have seen a lot of programmes about law on television.
- My subject teacher said I should do this.
- I had a bad teacher.
- That part of the course was boring.
- It's a long time since we covered that topic.
- I've forgotten.
- I want to heal the sick.
- Your department has a good reputation (unless you can expand on this).

It is far easier to give examples of bad answers than good! Good answers are personal to you – and must demonstrate the commitment, passion and enthusiasm that admissions staff are looking for. You will find examples of many more interview questions given in the books listed at the end of this chapter. Some of them also suggest possible ways of answering them!

AND MORE TIPS – FROM STUDENTS THIS TIME

'Before an interview practise answers to the more obviously likely questions. When you give your reasoning for choosing a course at a given university, be sure to give an example of something they offer that others do not. This is a way of proving that you have done your research properly.'

'Be sure that you remember exactly what you put on your personal statement. All three of my interviewers used it as a structure and based the interview around it.'

'Don't lie or exaggerate anything. You will be found out!'

'It is absolutely paramount to be sure that you want to be radiographer. If not, you will end up hating every minute of the course. You must also be able to convince admissions tutors that you have done some research into the work, so you need to spend some time observing practice and talking to radiographers.

'The two branches of the profession are very different and suit different people. Radiotherapists treat patients who have cancer and build up a relationship with them over several visits. Diagnostic radiographers see patients much more briefly – and possibly only once. Their work has more variety and ranges from taking basic X-rays in a clinic situation to working in the operating theatre or dealing with emergencies – with people who have potentially life-threatening injuries. You need to be able to convince the interviewers that you understand the difference and have chosen the branch that you are suited to.'

WHAT TO WEAR

If in doubt, go for 'smart casual'. There is no need to go out and buy an interview suit. Academic staff at HEIs are not likely to be wearing them either.

Students say:

'It really did not matter. I went to my two interviews wearing a shirt, trousers and black shoes. I saw some people who were wearing suits and others who were much more casual. The important thing is to wear something you feel comfortable in.'

'For my first two interviews I wore my school skirt and sweater. It doesn't look obviously like a school uniform as it has no badges or logos and I felt that it looked smart. By the third one I was really noticing what everyone else wore and saw that it didn't actually matter. Nobody was very formal. So from then on I wore smart jeans with a decent top. I think the key is to wear something that you are comfortable in and something that won't annoy the interviewer by being too extreme or in a very bright colour.'

AUDITIONS

If you apply for music or drama performance courses you will face much more than one interview. You will also have to audition. In general, but not exclusively, music candidates have one or more auditions on one day but drama applicants may have as many as four *recall* auditions (one is more usual – making a total of two).

Performance-based courses receive applications from very well-qualified students. Their teachers, who know how difficult it is to win places, would not recommend them otherwise. These are not the same type of course as those offered in some 'top' universities which are more academic even though they do contain a practical element. Competition for places at music conservatoires or drama schools which are members of the **Conference of Drama Schools** is intense.

Music

Expect a panel audition with two or more people at a music conservatoire. The audition could last between 15–30 minutes, although piano auditions at some places take 45 minutes. You will normally be expected to perform two contrasting pieces and these should demonstrate the full extent of your ability. Some conser-vatoires publish a list of pieces for you to choose from. The composers used vary but Bach, Boccherini, Haydn, Hoffmeister, Mozart and Vivaldi feature prominently.

Others give you a free choice. In this case your instrument or voice teacher will be able to advise you on what is suitable. Applicants for composition are often asked to send in advance copies of a set number of contrasting, fully notated pieces, preferably with recordings.

If your instrument is very large – for example a harp or double bass – you may be asked whether you would like the conservatoire to provide one for your audition.

In addition to your audition pieces you could expect to do any of the following:

- Play a further short solo piece which you will have been given a copy of one hour before your audition
- Complete short sight-reading exercises
- Improvise
- Complete technical tests including scales and arpeggios
- Have an aural skills assessment – often in a group of applicants completing the assessment at the same time.

These forms of assessment do vary from conservatoire to conservatoire, but you will be sent instructions telling you exactly what to expect and what you will need to prepare for in advance.

It is a good idea to arrive early for an audition as you will often be assigned an individual practice room in which to warm up for 25–30 minutes before your audition starts.

ADAM IS IN HIS FINAL YEAR OF A DEGREE COURSE, A BA IN ACTING AT THE GUILDFORD SCHOOL OF ACTING (GSA) – YOU CAN LOOK AT HIS WEBSITE, ADAMROOD.COM
GSA normally receives 1300 applications for 120 places.

The Head of Production from GSA visited Adam's sixth-form college to conduct a workshop with a group of students and auditioned them there. Adam was successful and received an invitation to a recall audition in Guildford. Immediately he knew that he wanted a place there. 'It was very friendly and welcoming – unlike some of the larger colleges. I felt at home.'

For the audition at his own college Adam had to prepare two speeches, each lasting two minutes. Some schools produce a list of audition pieces but Adam was free to choose his own provided that one was classical and one modern. He chose to do one from *Hamlet* and one from *Pitchfork Disney* by Philip Ridley. The recall audition began on a Friday evening and continued through the next day.

'On the Friday evening we had a three hour workshop with the principal and senior Acting tutors. There were about 20 of us and we worked in small groups on warm up exercises, improvisation, acting and movement. We were being assessed on talent - not just raw talent but also potential that could be developed at GSA, as well as the ability to work with a number of different people. On the Saturday morning we had one hour assessments in each of singing, dance and movement and voice. They were looking for strengths in at least two of these.

'At lunchtime some people were told that they had been unsuccessful and others were kept on for the afternoon. This was the time for physical and vocal appraisals - acting is a tough profession and the training is rigorous. Sometimes people are advised to get fitter or in rarer cases, have their tonsils removed due to potential vocal problems later on down the line. I was asked to improve my all round physical fitness.

'During the afternoon I also had a 20 minute one to one interview. The tutor went through my CV asking me questions on performances I had been in and people I had worked with. It was informal and friendly, more like a conversation than an interview. I was also asked to criticise other people's work and for my opinions on the best and worst pieces of theatre I had seen.

'I left, with the promise that I would know if I had been accepted within a week.'

Advice from Adam

'Be yourself completely and utterly. Don't put on an act or try to be what you think they want you to be. They want to see you as you are.

'Know your audition speeches inside out, back to front and upside down. That way there is no chance of freezing and drying up.

'Know the rest of the play, know about the playwright and the play's history. Apparently 50% of people at audition have only read the scene that contains their speech. This is because they select their speech from a monologue book and do no further reading. You will probably be asked questions on the character and the play. If I hadn't read the previous scene I would not have been able to respond when asked why Hamlet was feeling as he did.

'Be at a distance of at least five paces from the panel. The more distance you are willing to cover, the braver you look. But don't play to them. Behave as though you were on a stage performing to an audience. They need to see you working in that situation. Some people were asked to repeat their audition speeches and do some more work on them during the interview.

'Do your research. Find out about the school and know why you want to audition and train there. You will almost always be asked why you are auditioning for the school, so have an answer that is honest and genuine. "Your school is in the CDS (Conference of Drama Schools) so it must be good" shows naivety and that you have done no research whatsoever. "Guildford is a beautiful town, I like the way that your timetable is structured and I feel that your training has a lot to offer me. I really feel I could be at home here" is a much better response and shows good professional conduct and a willingness to learn.

'Drama Schools often advise you to have no help when preparing your audition speeches and that they want to see your individual work and interpretation. The fact is that an outside eye of someone that you trust - either a director or an actor - is very beneficial. They can help you see thoughts in a speech that you didn't even know existed. They will also point out vocal problems and involuntary and sometimes unnecessary movement during the speech.

'Most importantly, talk to the students. Find out what the course is really like. Ask them to be open and honest to you about the stronger and weaker elements of the school. Remember that, despite all the hype about getting in to a drama school you are actually going to have to spend three years of your life here, and you want a training that you feel will fully prepare you for the world of the performing arts, a world that is constantly changing and increasingly competitive.'

CHAPTER EIGHT
OFFERS AND REJECTIONS

Between October and March admissions tutors will decide whether or not to offer you a place. They might invite you to an interview or Open Day first, but neither of these is automatic. Offers (and rejections) can come quickly or take some time. *Please* don't get anxious if your friends seem to be getting replies before you do. It's not a bad sign. It could be due to all sorts of things – HEI policy and timing, number of applications received, admissions tutors' workload etc.

HEIs send their decisions to UCAS whose staff pass them to you. But you don't have to wait anxiously for the post. Use **Track**. Individual universities and colleges may also write to you telling you that they are going to offer you a place. But this information is not official until it is passed on to you by UCAS.

The decisions can be C – Conditional Offers, dependent on your getting certain exam grades, or U – Unconditional ones if you already have the grades. The offers can come at any time but you do not have to reply to any of them until you have had replies from all the HEIs. They have to make all their decisions by 9th May although UCAS asks them to do so if they can by 31st March. When you have all the decisions UCAS asks for your reply. You can reply by using **Track** or by contacting the UCAS Customer Service Unit.

Decision-making now passes to you. Your decisions are between F – Firm Acceptance, I – Insurance Acceptance and D – Decline. If you are in the lucky position of having received several offers you will now need to reject some. This is in fairness to other applicants who may now be offered the places you decide against.

It is very important to take great care when choosing between offers! You will have put a lot of thought into your original application. You will have chosen places where you thought you could be happy and whose entry requirements should be within your reach. Before you make your choice do double check with subject teachers whether they are still expecting you to get the same grades or whether they think you might do better or worse (they, and you, should have a pretty good idea of course, looking at your various module results). But there are problems every year. Some students accept one high offer – say AAB. They turn down two offers of BBC and go for a much lower insurance offer of CCC, thinking 'I'm safe. I will get these grades easily.' They then achieve BBC and immediately wish they had hung on to another one. Do ask for advice.

Ultimately, you may accept just one offer firmly (your Firm Acceptance). This means that you are committed to going to that HEI if it confirms that it has accepted you after the exam results. You may also make one Insurance Acceptance. Students often wonder whether it is worth accepting the second offer. Yes it is. If you don't get the results you need for your first choice you will have somewhere to go – somewhere you have already decided that you like (as opposed to making a new choice at the exam results stage). It is important to put as much thought into accepting your Insurance offer as for the Firm one. You would be committed to it, just as that HEI would have to honour its obligation to you. This is something applicants must be very clear about. You do not choose between the two offers at this stage. If your Firm Acceptance HEI accepts you then, it is to that one that you go. You can't suddenly think 'Oh, I'll take the other one instead. I think that I would like that place better now.'

Do not accept any Insurance offer unless you are sure that you would be happy at that HEI.

Unfortunately there is a third type of decision that you may receive. This is – Rejection.

What happens if you don't get any offers? Or if you receive some but decide to decline them?

From the end of February (26th February in 2008) to the end of the first week in July, UCAS will give you the chance to make one more application through a system known as **Extra**. If you are eligible to use **Extra** UCAS will automatically contact you and explain what to do. What happens is that a button named **Extra** will appear on the screen when you log on to **Track**. Use this and all will be explained. If you are a CUKAS applicant with no offers you will now be offered the opportunity to apply again through **Extra.**

Being eligible to use **Extra** means either:

- Not having received any offers
- Having received some but declined them (people do sometimes change their minds).
- Having cancelled some of the choices on the application.

USING EXTRA

You will need to get into the **Course Search** section of the UCAS website and look for courses that still have vacant places. They will be identified by being highlighted. You will be able to choose one and enter this choice through **Track**. The application is then sent to the HEI automatically. If you receive an offer you must make a decision in the same way as accepting or declining any other offer – as described earlier in this chapter.

If you are not made an offer within 21 days or decide to decline one that is made, your **Extra** button will show again on the screen and you may try again.

It is very, very important to put a lot of thought into an **Extra** decision. It is helpful to reconsider your options at this point and perhaps go for a less high-demand course. But there is the danger of clutching at straws here and grabbing a place simply because it is offered.

However, if you have the right predicted grades for top courses you should have received some offers by now and will not need **Extra**. Things can go wrong though, which is why both **Extra** and **Clearing** are receiving some coverage. It is also very likely that if you have applied for places on top courses you will not find **Extra** much help. You will have applied for competitive courses whose admissions tutors will have received a large number of applications. They are very unlikely to have any places up for grabs in the spring.

It could still be worth checking, but remember that you do not have to take a place offered at this stage. It could be worth waiting until August when a lot of places will become available. Why does this happen? Because:

- The Insurance places of people who got the right grades for their Firm Acceptance HEI become available. So do the places of applicants who were unfortunate and did not get their grades.

Admittedly, not all the places become available because admissions tutors nearly always offer more places than they have, earlier in the year, to allow for these factors.

- Some applicants achieve better grades than they expected and decide to withdraw from the system and try again for a higher status course for the following year.
- Some applicants decide that they do not want to go on to higher education after all.
- Others decide to take a gap year and arrange to have their places held open for the following year if they can.

So a number of places come back on the market.

 EXTRA TIPS

- Be prepared to be flexible
- Perhaps choose a different course
- Or an HEI you had not previously considered
- But think very carefully
- Get help and advice from staff at your school, college or your referee.

What if...

Suppose you don't find a place through **Extra** either? Then there is another safety net! UCAS operates **Clearing** during the summer when HEIs advertise their empty places with the grades required and students apply for them. Vacancies are published on the UCAS website (www.ucas. com/clearing). By arrangement with UCAS, *The Independent* and *The Independent on Sunday* also publish its official lists. Newspapers may bid to do this with UCAS. *The Independent* is usually the winner and in fact renewed their contract with UCAS in January 2008 for a three-year period. Other national newspapers produce their own listings at this time.

Clearing and what to do in mid-August when the results are out are described in Chapter 9.

CHAPTER NINE
RESULTS DAY

A t some point in the July or August after you have taken your exams you will get the results. Depending on your exam board you may receive them in the post or they may be sent to your school or college for staff there to distribute to you. Schools and colleges have different ways of doing this. Some use the simple but (to my mind) unkind method of putting lists up on notice boards for students to read. Not only can this take a little while if students are expecting results from more than one board but they have to scour the lists in the company of everyone else. At others, students receive their results in person and in private from a tutor, Head of Year or other appropriate person. Many schools and colleges have advisers present all day – maybe their own staff or advisers from the local careers or Connexions service – who can counsel students on their options.

If you have been around in mid-August in the last few years you cannot fail to have seen the breakfast television programmes on which some brave students open their envelopes in front of family, journalists – and viewers. You will get the impression from this that all exam results arrive on the same day. Not so. Scottish students normally get their Higher results on the second Tuesday in August – by post to their home addresses (although last year for the first time an online service was pioneered with varying degrees of success. Many students forgot their passwords or failed to log on for other reasons and had to wait until the next day after all.). A level students get their results on the third Thursday in August. However, students taking advanced Diploma courses, including the IB will have been quietly in possession of their results since July.

The reason for all the media hype on the A level results day is that these are the last of the results to be published. It is at this point that the official system to help those who have not got the grades they needed for their higher education places kicks in. It can't begin before then because all the results have to be known before HEIs can do their sums and see how many students have got their grades and how many will not be enrolling. Even then they can't be sure exactly how many places they have until all the students have made their decisions. Some may withdraw, decide to take a gap year or drop out all together. Some may have made applications simultaneously through different systems e.g. UCAS and CUKAS, UCAS and Art Foundation Course, UCAS and independent HEI…They now have to make their final choice and some more places might become vacant.

But – to go back a step – you receive your results and they are just what you needed. You have met the terms of your offer. What will you need to do? Answer – *absolutely nothing*. The HEI and UCAS will do that for you. You can go off to celebrate with your friends, let your parents ring all their friends, and wait for official confirmation of your acceptance to arrive.

If you have qualified for your first choice HEI you will receive official notification from UCAS and a welcome pack from the HEI. Even if you don't quite make the grades you may still be in at your first choice.

WHAT IF YOU DON'T GET THE GRADES?

Then there is the UCAS **Clearing** system to help you. BUT you may not need it.

It does not necessarily follow that if you didn't meet the grades your Firm Choice HEI will reject you. It may still accept you if you are a grade or two down. The admissions tutors offered you a place originally because they thought you would make a good student. If they have spare capacity they might fit you in. If the course is full (and it is common practice to offer more than the number of places that exist in order to reach targets), they can't do so. But other things being equal, most of them would prefer to be kind to a student they have already selected than put the place up for grabs and get applications at this late stage from people they have never heard of.

If they can't take you, you will now be automatically considered by your Insurance HEI. Rather than assume that you will need to use **Clearing** it is worth checking the situation with both HEIs. Their phone lines will be jammed by other students in the same position from the minute they open so you will need to be patient. If neither can accept you, you will automatically be entered into **Clearing**. UCAS will send you a **Clearing** passport and a set of instructions.

Clearing

UCAS says that 30,000 people gain a place during **Clearing** every year. It also says that if you are flexible and you have reasonable exam results, there is still a good chance you will find another course.

An interactive **Clearing** course search appears on the UCAS website on the day of the Scottish exam results for Scottish vacancies only. So, if you are interested in Scottish HEIs only, this service may interest you. But if you want to look at UK-wide vacancies you will have to wait for the full UK **Clearing** service to open.

Who may use Clearing?

You will be eligible for **Clearing** if one of the following applies (provided that you haven't withdrawn your application):

- You are holding no offers
- Your offers have not been confirmed (i.e. your grades are not the ones that were required)
- You have declined your offers or have not responded by the due date
- Your offers have not been confirmed and you have declined any alternative offers from the same university or college
- You applied after 30th June (12th June for Route B Art and Design courses).

How does it work?

Once you are eligible for **Clearing**, UCAS will send you a **Clearing** passport: a form you use to secure a place. If an HEI is willing to consider your application, it will ask for the **Clearing** number that is printed on the passport (you can also find it on **Track**). If the HEI that you apply to through **Clearing** decides to offer you a place it will ask you to send your passport – direct to the HEI, not to UCAS.

How do you know where there are vacant places? They are advertised on the UCAS website and also in *The Independent*.

You can now use **Track** at ucas.com to keep a close eye on your progress. If you are accepted on to a course, the HEI will get in touch with UCAS and then that information will be displayed on **Track**.

However, obtaining a place doesn't just happen. You would have to get going immediately and set to work to find one. You would do so by ringing HEIs direct (it wouldn't be easy – at what would after all be a very upsetting time – but thousands of students do so every August).

You don't need to know all the fine detail of **Clearing** at this stage – and in any case every quality newspaper in the UK devotes pages and pages to this topic every July and August (I have written a number of them). Also, we hope that you won't need **Clearing**, don't we? So what follows is an outline.

At most HEIs students' calls are made to a **Clearing** help desk which is run by specially trained staff. Some are university administrative staff but many are students who are being paid to work at this time. Some of them have been **Clearing** entrants themselves and understand what callers are going through. They take a few basic details and then may be empowered to offer a place, or more likely pass students on to members of academic staff. They too are usually very sympathetic. Many have teenage sons or daughters who have just had their results. After asking you some questions (the sort you had to have answers to earlier in the year – 'Why this course?' etc. – they might offer you a place. Or they might offer you a place on an alternative but related course. If you are interested, you can provisionally accept it and might then be invited to an Open Day.

There are some wise precautions to take at this time, like not accepting the first offer made to you. Once your UCAS passport has been sent to one HEI – it's the end of the line. You have made a final choice. But all this would be covered in the media and repeated by advisers at the time.

You can see from all this that it is imperative to be available in person in August and plan your summer holiday around exam results day. You might have to deal with admissions tutors and would need to make some pretty important decisions. A lot of tutors have stories to recount of parents or friends calling on behalf of someone who is away somewhere with the suntan cream – and who cannot answer any questions!!

Other plans?

OK. That was **Clearing**. It's not for everybody. It is given so much media hype and publicity that it's tempting to think that it is the only option. It isn't. And it isn't for many people who want to get a place on a top course. Very few of them turn up in **Clearing** – although some surprising ones do every year. The **Clearing** option, as UCAS admits, is for students who are prepared to be flexible in their choices.

If you badly, badly wanted to do a particular course is it not worth giving up one year of your life to try again? I'm talking about re-taking exams and applying again. This isn't for everyone either. As with most choices there are advantages and disadvantages. The most obvious is that some HEIs would expect you to get better results than students who are sitting A levels (or equivalent) for the first time. Could you do that?

How do you know which HEIs might ask for higher grades a second time around? If the information is readily available – and do look first – on their websites or in their UCAS **Entry Profile**, you can get the answer quite quickly. If not, *ask them*. Being a belt and braces sort of person if it were my application I would do so anyway (!) through a short letter (remember that admissions tutors are very, very busy at this time of year) saying that I had seen that their policy was to discourage/accept re-takes/ask for higher grades the second time round and could they please confirm that this was still the policy as I badly wanted to go there.

If the HEIs that you chose originally don't like re-take applicants or push the grades up to ridiculous levels (and some can hardly go much higher already) then go back to your original shortlist and see whether any that you considered then might be suitable.

Policies really do vary between individual departments. There is never an HEI-wide policy. I have been told personally when making enquiries on behalf of students that some course admissions tutors simply don't want re-take candidates and by others that any person who is very keen to study a particular subject should have the determination to have a second go at getting there.

Now for the downside. Just as **Clearing** is not right for everyone, not everyone is suited to re-takes. It's not easy to go over the same ground. In fact some students decide to take an intensive one-year course in one new subject, taking AS modules in January and A2s in June. This does mean hard work but for some it can be the right choice. If you first check that one of your previous subjects is not essential this could be a good plan.

However, there are questions you would have to ask yourself before booking a place on a re-take course:

- Can I really do better?
- Were these the grades I was expected to get?
- Or did something go wrong?
- Were there genuine medical or family reasons that affected my exam performance?
- Did I do enough revision?
- Have I asked my subject teachers for an honest opinion?
- Is there something else I would be happy to do t at is achievable with my current grades?

And if you did decide to re take some subjects:

- Would it be better to re-take two and start one new subject?
- Where am I going to study for re-takes?

What if you change your mind?

Suppose your grades were even better than you expected and you wished you had applied for a course with higher entry requirements? What if you now wanted a place on a 'better' course?

Officially nothing can be done. That at least is the UCAS position. The rules state firmly that candidates are committed to their CF and CI HEIs. They accepted these conditions when they applied (not that they had any choice!). It would upset the system tremendously if lots of students started shopping around at results time – hence the rules, but in the real world we all know that a small number of students manage to change HEIs every year. The trick is that you would have to get your original HEI to release you so that you can tell others that you are not firmly committed anywhere. In practice they usually do not try to hang on to students in this position. After all no one wants reluctant students on their courses.

However, you would have to be sure of an offer from the new HEI first. And bearing in mind that everyone everywhere is under pressure at this time of year answers may not be so quick to come.

Perhaps a gap year might be a better alternative? You could travel, learn a new skill, work to earn some money to help finance higher education – submitting a new UCAS application as early as possible in September. But once again you should try to get some confirmation before doing so that your current grades would be acceptable for the course that you want and at the place where you hope to do it.

N.B. If you now found that you hoped to change to a different course at the same HEI, UCAS and rules do not enter in to it. This would be a matter for negotiation between you and the HEI.

You can see that for many students August is a time for rethinking. But you would not have to do this all on your own. Advice would be available. Many schools and colleges stay open at this time of year. Subject teachers come back from their holidays in time to be around to help their students. Another excellent source of help is the nearest careers or Connexions service whose advisers are there throughout the **Clearing** period. You should be able to make one or more appointments to someone who can discuss *all* the options with you. Careers advisers are trained to discuss all the alternatives – course choice, re takes, gap year – even employment. What is more, their advice is completely impartial.

CHAPTER TEN

POSTSCRIPT

ON LEAVING A TOP UNIVERSITY OR COURSE

This book is about gaining a place on the course you want. But it pays to look ahead as well…

Having a good degree from a good HEI is not enough! Too often careers advisers see students who think that the world owes them a living because they have been to a high status university. Not so!

Many jobs are open to students with degrees in any subject. Employers offering these are not interested in an in-depth knowledge of third world development or Shakespeare's plays. What they are looking for is intellectual ability (which means that graduates will be fast learners in new situations and will bring with them the ability to solve problems and create change) *plus what are known as soft or transferable skills*. These are personal skills that can be transferred to most working environments. **You do not gain them simply by working hard and getting a respected degree.**

What are they?

Exact definitions – and order of popularity vary from year to year but these are the ones that keep cropping up:

- Ability to cope under pressure
- Adaptability
- Commercial awareness
- Communication, both verbal and written
- Initiative
- Leadership

- Numeracy
- Persuasive skill
- Problem solving ability
- Self reliance
- Teamwork.

Obviously, many jobs do require a specific degree subject. However, employers in these areas also look for the above qualities. Engineers, accountants, scientists etc. also need to be able to lead, manage, communicate and work with other people!

Some employers even look back to A level/Higher/Diploma grades, and in addition to a specific class of degree ask also for a certain set of grades or a number of UCAS points, as in the case of two companies quoted below.

Some employers' comments

Applicants for positions as IT consultants should have:

- 300 UCAS points
- At least a 2:1 degree in an IT, engineering or scientific subject

and should be:

- Excellent written and oral communicators
- Strong team players
- Confident
- Proactive
- Able to work on their own in initiative
- Able to work alone
- Able to manage many work streams in parallel.

PA consulting group candidates should possess:

- A 2:1 degree in any subject
- 320 UCAS points
- Paid or voluntary work experience.

❝ We look for people with more than just excellent academics. We need individuals who are passionate about something outside their studies, who have some work experience and a strong interest in business and technology.❞

ACCENTURE (INTERNATIONAL MANAGEMENT CONSULTANTS)

❝ We welcome applications from all academic disciplines. More importantly, we seek people who demonstrate strong leadership skills, creativity, communication and analytical thinking.❞

PROCTER & GAMBLE

❝ We welcome graduates from a wide range of university courses. Academic discipline is less important than the personal qualities an individual brings with them. However, a strong interest in and appreciation of finance is important. Whatever the background, it is intellect, personality and zest for life that the firm values most.❞

GOLDMAN SACHS (INVESTMENT BANK)

❝ Tesco is interested in graduates from any discipline, who combine people management and analytical skills with the character to succeed in a constantly changing business. Full of fresh ideas, they need to demonstrate leadership to become a senior manager and to show energy, enthusiasm and passion for the Tesco business.❞

TESCO

So, what they want are students who have taken part in a range of extra-curricular activities and have work experience – either in a term time job or during the vacations. Voluntary experience is also useful.

When you complete your UCAS or other higher education application you will be using some of your extra-curricular activities to prove certain things to admissions tutors. As you have read, not all of them take these into consideration. Employers will do so.

It is very, very important to make good use of your time in higher education, to continue or take up new activities, and leave as a rounded person as well as a graduate.

Two books by Trotman are written on this subject:

What can I do with an arts degree?
What can I do with a social sciences degree?

Obviously, they are meant for graduates whose degree subject does not apparently point in a particular direction but both contain chapters on transferable skills which will be useful to graduates from vocational courses too.

USEFUL SOURCES OF INFORMATION

Books

Boehm, Claus and Lees-Spalding, Jenny. *Student Book 2008*, 2008.

Burnett, James. *Getting into Art and Design Courses*, 2008.

Burnett, James. *Getting into Dental School*, 2007.

Burnett, James. *Getting into Medical School*, 2008.

Burnett, James. *Getting into Physiotherapy Courses*, 2008.

Di Clemente, Mario. *Getting into Veterinary School*, 2007.

Heap, Brian. *Choosing Your Degree Course and University*, 2008.

Heap, Brian. *Degree Course Offers 2009*, 2008.

Lancer, Natalie. *Getting into Oxford and Cambridge*, 2008.

Smith, Katie. *Getting into Business and Management Courses*, 2007.

Waterstone, Maya. *Getting into Psychology Courses*, 2008.

All by Trotman.

Trotman Publishing in association with UCAS. *How to Complete Your UCAS Application 2009 Entry*, Trotman Publishing, 2008.

UCAS, *The Big Guide 2009*, UCAS, 2008.

The UCAS Directory 2008

Virgin, *The Virgin Alternative Guide to British Universities*, Virgin Books, 2007.

Websites

www.admissions.ox.ac.uk

www.bmat.org.uk

www.cam.ac.uk/admissions/undergraduate

www.hesa.ac.uk

www.lnat.ac.uk

www.studentuk.com

www.thegooduniversityguide.org.uk

www.tsa.cambridgeassessment.org.uk

www.ucas.com

www.ukcat.ac.uk

www.wikijob.co.uk (careers site)

Telephone numbers

CUKAS Customer Service Helpline

0871 468 0470, Monday to Friday, 08:30–18:00.

UCAS Customer Service Helpline

0871 468 0468, Monday to Friday, 08:30–18:00.